Home
Schooling 101

A guide to getting started.

The step-by-step guide to getting started, choosing curriculum, creating lesson plans, and staying the course.

ERICA ARNDT

This book is dedicated to all of the beloved parents who have committed their lives to educating their children at home.

Thank you to all of my readers for your constant support.
Without you, Confessions of a Homeschooler would not exist!

I would like to give a special thank you to my mom, and co-editor, for a lifetime of support. And for taking the time to read every last word.

Table of Contents

Chapter 1

You've Decided to Homeschool... Now What?

So you've finally decided to homeschool...but have no clue where to get started? Just the mere thought of homeschooling can be a very daunting task. Delving into the unknown can also create an element of self-doubt that fills your mind right off the bat. That coupled with an overwhelming task of choosing and gathering curriculum, creating lesson plans, organizing supplies, and teaching multiple grade levels can be quite disheartening.

But don't worry, in this book it is my intention to offer you a step by step practical guide that will help you to get started and continue on in your homeschooling journey. I will help guide you through all of the steps to getting started, choosing and gathering curriculum, creating effective lesson plans, scheduling your day, organizing your home, staying the course, and more!

As you may have heard already, there is no one right way to homeschool. This book is by no means a rigid set of rules that must be followed exactly. Instead it is a tool to provide you with the means to get started in your journey. Take from it what makes sense for your family, and alter that which needs to be changed to fit the unique needs of your homeschool.

So let's get started shall we?

Get a vision!

The best way to begin your homeschooling journey is to start with the basics. First I suggest that you start off by creating a vision for your homeschooling journey. I think you will find you have all of the tools necessary to guide you through this journey if you seek God's will for your homeschool, and take some time to pray for direction.

By creating a vision statement for why you are homeschooling, you'll have a backbone to fall upon when doubt and indecision creep in. In the Homeschooling Vision Worksheet (See Appendix) you will define your homeschooling goals, what you are striving towards, and why you are choosing to homeschool.

Once you've laid this foundation you will be more prepared for the trials that will follow.

Why are you homeschooling?

Beginning with basics, ask yourself this question…why are you homeschooling? Is this something you feel called to do, or are there other reasons motivating you towards this journey? Taking some time to list the reasons for your choice to homeschool is a great way to solidify your decision. Writing it down will also help remind you why you chose this direction and help get you back on track if you start to lose focus or get discouraged.

I highly encourage you to write down your reasons for choosing to homeschool and keep it somewhere handy so you can refer back to it whenever you find yourself doubting your decision.

Did we make the right choice?

Should I have put my children in school?

Am I teaching my children enough?

Are they missing something by being taught at home?

Unfortunately one of the biggest issues homeschoolers can face is the indecision and doubt factor. Of course we all want what is best for our children's education, and if things aren't going as expected we need a reminder of why we chose this path to start with. Knowing what the goals for our homeschool are, we can adjust what we're doing so we're moving toward those goals and not toward what someone else tells us we should be doing.

Know *your* state laws

While you don't have to be a lawyer to homeschool, you will at the very least need a basic knowledge of your state laws and requirements for homeschooling. Each state is different, so you'll want to make sure that you are following your specific state requirements.

The best place to learn about your state's homeschooling laws is by visiting the Homeschool Legal Defense Association (www.hslda.org). They have current homeschooling information, laws, and general information on getting started as well.

Here are some of the things you'll want to find out:

- At what age is a student required to start formal school?

- What are the requirements for attendance? (I.e. How many days per year are you required to do school.)

- What is the amount of hours required per year?

- What kind of records do I have to keep each year?

- What subjects do I have to teach?

- Is there a certain curriculum required?

- What requirements or qualifications must I have to teach my children at home?

- What is the age of attendance? (Most states require school attendance by 6 years of age, but again states may vary.)

- Is a Notice of Intent to homeschool required? If so when and where do you need to submit it? (There is a Notice of Intent form in the complimentary Homeschooling Lesson Planner that comes with this book.)

- Is Standardized Testing required? If so, when and where do you send results?

- Are you required to "withdraw" from public school? If your students are currently enrolled in a school district you may be required to officially withdraw them from the school, then submit your notice of intent to homeschool prior to starting.

As you can see there are some basic things you will need to find out prior to beginning your homeschooling journey, so please take some time to learn about your specific state requirements.

When should I start school?

One frequently asked question regarding homeschooling is when to start. A few states require you start keeping records for schooling at the age of 5 but most start at the age of 6. Aside from state requirements, doing school with children younger than the state specified start age is entirely up to you.

When starting to introduce more formal educational activities with students keep in mind the "big picture". If it's not your goal to graduate your child early, then there's really no reason to push school on them too soon.

If you think your child is ready and you are eager to start, there's no harm in starting to initiate more structured activities with a toddler, but be careful not to push them too hard, or force an activity on them. Doing so can result in a child who is less than eager to learn via homeschooling.

That said, first time moms may still wonder what they can do to help put their toddlers on the right track. Playing fun games with them, allowing them to experiment with art media, and reading to them often are all wonderful ways to encourage an early love for learning.

One thing to consider is that you might already be doing a form of school with your toddler and just not realize it. By telling them what something is called or being more specific in your speech such as saying "Put on your blue coat" you are teaching them. If your child is expressing an interest in something specific encourage them in their pursuit.

> **What Can I Do?**
>
> "Children as young as 1.5 to 3 years old can be having fun with board books, gross motor skill activities, nursery songs, rhymes, and a lot of reading with their parents."

What can I do to get my child ready for school?

Children as young as 1.5 to 3 years old should be having fun with board books, gross motor skill activities, nursery songs, rhymes, and a lot of reading with their parents. Keep this time focused on learning through having fun, and let your child help guide the activities. If they're tired, frustrated, or bored stop the activity and try again later. Make time for activities that work on fine motor skills right now too. Some ideas include transferring objects using tongs or tweezers, playing with Play-Doh, painting, cutting, and lacing cards.

These types of activities will help tremendously when they need to use those fine motor muscles for writing.

You will most likely want to start more structured educational activities when your student reaches the age of 5-6. You can introduce something formal like a full kindergarten curriculum. If your child isn't quite ready you can also start off with something a little more structured, but not quite as aggressive such as a K4 kindergarten.

As I stated before, you will want to be familiar with your state homeschool laws to make sure you are following the required amount of school based on the age of your child. Aside from that you'll want to base your decision on the readiness of your unique student.

How do I know what to teach?
(a.k.a. Am I doing enough?)

One of the most frequently asked questions is how to know what to teach? Of course you can use the chart in chapter 2 as a guide, but ultimately you *(and your state requirements)* will dictate what you teach each year.

That can leave a lot of flexibility for homeschoolers, which is a blessing and a curse. Unfortunately many homeschoolers spend half of their time worrying whether or not they're teaching enough, or conversely if they're trying to cram too much in.

As you progress with your homeschooling journey, you will learn how much your family can reasonably cover in any given year. However if you are just starting out there are a few resources that can help guide you in your yearly topic suggestion. One such document is the "Scope & Sequence". Most major curriculum companies will publish a scope and sequence for varying grade levels which can be helpful when starting out.

There are also Common Core Standards that most public schools follow. Keep in mind as a homeschooler, unless mandated by the state, you are not required to follow any of these. However, they can be useful tools to help you get started.

As a matter of fact, I might encourage you NOT to stick to a certain scope and sequence unless it makes you feel better (or is required by your state). Instead take a quick look back at your vision statement. Taking into consideration the goals you set forth, pick subject matter and curriculum that will help you achieve those specific goals in your home.

Keep in mind what will best prepare your students for adulthood and their career interests. The scope and sequence can provide a nice starting point for you. However you'll soon discover that it doesn't matter at what age your student learns a specific skill, but instead how well they learn it, the end result is what matters.

Think about the big picture.

This is where NOT comparing your homeschool or your students to others comes into full play. And my advice to you…"Ignore the Joneses".

You all know them; they're the perfect homeschooling family. The Joneses have successfully homeschooled 10 children, all of whom are absolutely enthralled with learning at home. They sew they're own clothes…from the wool they spun before breakfast…from the sheep they've raised by hand since birth. They all play an instrument to excellence, forming an entire family musical ensemble. They travel the globe speaking at events and performing live. They all speak 7 different languages. And their youngest is an award winning composer at the age of 4.

But no matter how perfect another homeschooling family may appear, I'm here to tell you that no family is perfect, except the one that is obeying God's calling.

Do not allow yourself to be discouraged because you have fallen into the trap of comparison. The reality of it is that everyone learns at different levels. Each of us has different needs, learning styles, and teaching styles. Contrary to popular belief, not all homeschoolers are several grades above their age level. Your children may be above the national standard, or right on grade level academically speaking and that is okay. They may even have delays or special needs, again it is okay. They may be ahead in math, but delayed in reading…yep, it's still okay.

Let me say that again.

"It's okay."

Every one of our children is different and the beauty of homeschooling is that it allows us to cater to the unique needs of our children. There is no need to compare your family with the "Joneses".

Instead pray about what God wants you to teach your children each year. Focus on your previously set vision and goals for your homeschool. Instead of cramming in facts to complete a book by the end of the year, teach topics to mastery. And absolutely invest in your child's own interests whenever you can!

Teach your children to love learning, and to work hard.

Count the cost

Homeschooling is one of the most self-sacrificial career choices out there and it will take a lot of time and dedication on your part. As homeschoolers we're with our children 24/7, we are called to train them, have patience with them, guide them through the good and bad, and be there through the thick and the thin.

If we're not careful we can fall into the trap of self-doubt, we can compare ourselves and our children to others, get discouraged by daily trials, and even face criticism from family and friends. But there is a flip side to this as well. You will also reap the rewards of a child learning to read, or watch them figure out something new on their own for the first time.

As a homeschooler you are investing in your child one of the most important things, your time. By teaching your children, you become the primary influence in their lives. You have the rare opportunity to deal with issues immediately, and teach your children morals, values, and character traits.

Let's be honest here for a minute. Homeschooling isn't for sissies, and homeschooling isn't easy. You will have wonderfully joyful days, and days that are tough. Your children will love it, and hate it at times. You might even love it and hate it at times. But the long term results will be eternal, and that reward can't be beat.

Rules & discipline

One of the things people tend to overlook when starting out with homeschooling is the need for some type of organized discipline. Both students and parents can be so excited to start that they overlook this necessity. By outlining the expectations for your homeschool and home, you will save yourself and your children from much heartache.

We've all gone through it, the beginning "homeschooling honeymoon." Everyone is excited to start, and looking forward to all of the fun they're about to have. You as the homeschooling parent have researched, planned, and prepared a year's worth of fun activities. You'll find yourself excited to impart all of your new found wisdom onto your beautiful children.

Unfortunately after about the first week or so the excitement can start to fade. Students and parents realize that they are actually required to do work that it isn't all fun and games as they originally dreamed.

And the truth is homeschooling can be fun, and it creates a wonderful bond between parent and child. But it is also hard work. Just as in a regular school setting, there are certain tasks that need to be done. Having defined your homeschooling goals in step one will greatly help in this area. You will know when it's okay to let something go, and when it is time to teach your children what it means to be diligent and hard working.

Prior to starting your homeschool year, I highly suggest creating a basic set of rules. Keep them basic and easy to remember. If needed, list some pre-planned consequences for broken rules to help alleviate any pressure on the homeschooling parent to come up with a discipline on the fly. If one of your children breaks the rule, refer to your pre-planned chart for the discipline.

On the opposite side of the consequences chart, I also suggest you create some type of rewards as well. Making good choices, doing your best, being diligent, are all character traits that we want to encourage. You don't want to constantly focus on negative behavior, but instead encourage and reward positive behavior.

In the Appendix, you will find a link to download our household rule chart as well as a behavior discipline chart. Feel free to use these charts as a starting point, or create your own based on the needs of your family.

> "Many are the plans in a person's heart, but it is the LORD's purpose that prevails."
>
> ~Proverbs 19:21

Creating a schedule

Another step in having a successful homeschooling routine is to create a workable schedule. This is not something that has to be written in stone, but having a schedule will help guide you through your day, week, and ultimately homeschooling year. Seek the Lord when making these plans as well and He will guide you. "Many are the plans in a person's heart, but it is the LORD's purpose that prevails." ~Proverbs 19:21.

Kids tend to thrive on consistency and structure and having a daily schedule will help keep everyone focused and on task. It can be a simple routine such as breakfast, school, lunch, school, chores, free time, dinner, and bed time. Or it can be more detailed to include extracurricular activities and the like. As you determine your schedule, make sure it is realistic for your family. Share the schedule with your children, and then hang it somewhere visible in the home. You can be as rigid or flexible as you need to be here, but at least you'll have a general plan to shoot for. Keeping the schedule is up to you.

The other part includes learning to be flexible. If there's an amazing display on Egypt at your local museum, take the day off and go! Chores and meals and everything else will get done later. One major advantage to homeschooling is that we have the flexibility to venture away from our "plan" and actually enjoy life with our children. *And hey, we can always make up school on Saturday. Your kids will love that!*

Team work

As we've already discussed, homeschooling will take up quite a bit of your time. Unfortunately, that doesn't mean that all of your other household duties will magically disappear. Creating an environment where the entire family pitches in to keep the home running smoothly is an essential part of your homeschooling journey. It also prevents the entire load that comes with running a household from falling onto one person.

Creating an atmosphere where the whole family is working as a team helps teach children responsibility. It will teach them how to care for others, be a good steward over what God has blessed them with, and gain a sense of worth and belonging to the family unit.

Need some help organizing your daily tasks? Download my free Chore Chart found at my website under "Mom Tips".

Chapter 2

Choosing Curriculum

Now that you've prepared yourself and your family for homeschooling, and familiarized yourself with state law, it's time to get into the logistics of homeschooling. One thing that has helped me the most in our homeschooling journey is to plan ahead.

While I know several families who choose to do school year round, we choose to take summer breaks each year. I use that time off to gather all of my curriculum, organize supplies, make lists of things we need, and get all of my lesson plans into my homeschooling software. However you choose to organize your year, I highly suggest making some time to prepare for each year prior to beginning.

Knowing that you're prepared for your year greatly reduces your stress level while in school. And it's much easier than trying to fly by the seat of your pants every day. Planning ahead helps keep chaos at bay, and also allows you to feel like you're actually accomplishing things that need to be done.

It also gives you the freedom to take breaks without feeling guilty. With a schedule you won't be panicking about getting behind. You'll know when you can and can't take a day off for that great exhibit at the local museum.

Obviously when starting to homeschool, one of the first things you'll need to do is choose your curriculum. While researching and choosing curriculum can seem like a daunting task, as you go through this book I hope you'll find helpful tips and pointers that will make the task more manageable.

Decide on subjects

Before setting out to choose curriculum, one of the first things I like to do is list the subjects we want to cover for the year. In my collection of homeschool planning forms *(See Appendix)*, I have created a curriculum sheet where I list all of the subjects that I plan to use for each student. This step is extremely helpful to complete prior to researching curriculum.

Please keep in mind that the subject lists below are not legal requirements *(check your state law),* they are merely a guide to help you get started choosing which subjects to do for each grade level.

* Indicates optional subjects for that grade.

** If you live in the United States of America, most states will also require that you do a certain amount of instruction in the Constitution of the United States each year.

Subject Guide

Kindergarten	1st & 2nd	3rd – 5th
Bible	Bible	Bible
Phonics/Reading	Reading	Reading
Math	Math	Math
Handwriting	Handwriting	Handwriting
* Art	Spelling	Spelling
* Social Studies	English/Language	English/Grammar
* Science	Social Studies	History/Geography
	Science/Health	Science/Health
	* Art	Writing
	* Music	* Art
	* PE	* Foreign Language
	** US History	* Literature
		* Music
		* PE
		* Typing
		** US History

6th – 8th	High School
Bible	If you are homeschooling a high school student, I highly recommend taking a look at college entrance requirements prior to setting your schedule for the year. Even if your child may not attend a formal college this will help you assess what classes and credits are typically required of a high school level degree.
Reading	
Math	
Handwriting	
Spelling	
English/Grammar	
History/Civics	
Science/Health	
Writing	
* Art	
* Foreign Language	
* Literature	
* Music	
* PE	
* Typing	
** US History	
* Speech/Debate	

Research curriculum

Once you have decided which subjects you will cover for the year it's time to start the process of researching curriculum. I will typically continue with curriculum that has been working for us, but will research new curriculum for things that need to be changed. If you're new to homeschooling, this stage will probably take the longest in your planning process.

One of my favorite places to go to get opinions on curriculum is www.HomeschoolReviews.com. This is a website where other homeschoolers share their

> "If any of you lacks wisdom, you should ask God, who gives generously to all without finding fault, and it will be given to you."
> ~ *James 1:5*

thoughts as well as list pros and cons for many different curricula. Reading reviews from other homeschoolers can be extremely helpful in deciding which curriculum will best fit your family. And again, seek God in your choices for each year. "If any of you lacks wisdom, you should ask God, who gives generously to all without finding fault, and it will be given to you." ~ *James 1:5*.

One thing I would like to point out is that after several years of homeschooling, I don't think I've found a curriculum that is absolutely perfect for us. While there are tons of different styles of curriculum, I don't think there's that "perfect" curriculum that fits every single need. However by reading reviews and trying different things, you should be able to find something that works for your family. You might have to modify it some and that's okay, homeschooling has a lot of flexibility and you are in charge. **Remember you control the curriculum; not the other way around!**

Homeschooling Methods

With homeschooling becoming an increasingly popular choice, several different approaches to homeschooling have also emerged. You're free to follow one specific style, blend them together, or create your own learning environment that works best for your family.

Here is a brief overview of the different methods of home education:

Traditional Method

Using curriculum that is similar to what is used in public school along with its more traditional grading system. This is commonly referred to as bringing traditional school into your home.

Classical Education Method

Classical education is based on a three-part process of training your mind. The grammar stage (the memorization stage), Logic Stage (The "why" stage), and Rhetoric Stage (Students learn to apply the knowledge gained in the previous two stages). This method is best described by Susan Wise Bauer. Visit her website at www.welltrainedmind.com for more information.

Charlotte Mason Method

Charlotte Mason developed a three-pronged educational approach centered around atmosphere, discipline, and life teaching. You can learn more about this at the Charlotte Mason website.

Eclectic Method

An eclectic approach to homeschooling is where the family takes bits and pieces of various different methods to form their own unique homeschooling environment.

Montessori Method

The Montessori Method is based on the idea that learning should be a natural, self-directed process. It is also commonly referred to as child-led learning. You can learn more about this method at the Montessori website.

Unschooling

Unschooling is another child-led type of approach to homeschooling. It is also commonly referred to as "natural Learning", "experience-based learning", or "independent learning." Unschooling homes typically let their current interests dictate what they choose to study, incorporating traditional subjects as they go.

Personally I prefer a more eclectic approach to homeschooling, meaning that I like to incorporate several different styles depending on the subject. For example, I tend to stick to more traditional methods for core subjects like math, English, and reading. But I also like to think out of the box for things like science, literature, and history. We also enjoy blending in unit studies wherever they might fit in.

Before boxing yourself into a specific learning style, consider being open to different types of learning as based on how they fit the needs and goals for your homeschool.

Again, make sure you are controlling your style, and not letting a certain style control you.

Let's start researching curriculum

The way I like to start researching curriculum, is to take the first topic for my oldest child. You'll immediately discover that there is literally a plethora of curriculum available for every subject out there and it can be easily overwhelming.

As you research, start writing down your top picks on a curriculum form such as the "Our Curriculum" form, (See

Appendix). Fill out the subjects you'll be covering, the curriculum you have chosen for a particular subject. If you are undecided leave it blank, or list a few of the curricula you are considering for that subject. You'll also want to note the cost of the curriculum if purchased new or the best online price you can receive including shipping costs.

This form will greatly aid you when actually ordering your curriculum from an online website or from a used curriculum fair. We will discuss these options in the next chapter titled "Gathering Curriculum".

Keep in mind the needs of your students as well as yourself when looking at various curriculum types. You'll find that there are a variety of options when picking curriculum. Some are referred to as "boxed" meaning that the work is done for you. Your job is to pull out the curriculum and just follow the directions. Others are a little more flexible and more of a guide for you to follow. Those types will take more preparation time on your part as you decide what to include in your lessons.

I like to include a variety of prepared curriculum, as well as some units that I can tailor for our family. This takes some of the burden off of me in preparing our year, but also allows me freedom to make school more fun with the more elective type subjects.

I like to use "boxed" curriculum for our core studies, then choose more flexible things for electives. With the core work off of my plate, I have more time to create more exciting hands-on units for some of the other subjects. Take a few minutes to decide what you prefer to spend more or less time planning and choose curriculum that fits those needs.

As you are researching your curricula, keep in mind what best fits your family. Try to narrow it down between your top two to three curricula choices. If possible discuss the pros and cons of these with your spouse or another homeschooling friend to get a different perspective.

Is the curriculum independent or teacher lead?

Make sure you have a blend of styles so that you are not overwhelmed with highly intensive teaching types of curriculum. Having a nice mix of these allows you to direct one student to do something more independent while working one-on-one with another student at the same time. It also teaches your child to learn to work independently as well. Curriculum styles run the gamut from scripted lessons that tell you exactly what to say to your students, to more informally organize curriculum that is highly dependent upon the teacher to organize and decide how to disseminate information to students.

What's the cost?

If cost is a factor for your family, as it is in most homeschools, make sure that the curriculum you choose is in line with your budget. Don't get swept into thinking that expensive = better. There are numerous budgetary options when homeschooling, and there are even websites dedicated to homeschooling for free. You can find quite a few free homeschooling resources with a simple internet search.

Student style

There are the 3 basic styles when referring to student learning styles. **Visual** (learning through seeing), **Auditory** (learning through hearing), and **Kinesthetic** (learning through moving, doing & touching). While each person is unique in their preferred learning style, I prefer to pick a curriculum that will appeal to all of these styles together to create a better-rounded learning environment. If your student is primarily an auditory learner you'll still want to incorporate more visual and kinesthetic lessons into their day so that they're not only learning to understand things in new ways, but also to fully experience them. You will also want to keep in mind student style, especially if you have a special needs learner.

Teacher style

As I mentioned previously, there are several different teaching styles as well, and I'm a firm believer that your teaching style is just as important as your student's learning style. Personally, I'm much more traditional / eclectic in my homeschooling approach. Eclectic just means that we gather different curricula for different subjects as needed. I think the best advice here is to start with what you feel "comfortable" with and then be flexible. As you go through a curriculum, if something's just not working, search for other options until you find what works best for you and your child together.

The best curriculum out there is the one you'll actually use. Remember, a curriculum might look great, but if it takes up too much time and energy on your part, you'll soon find yourself procrastinating by putting off the lessons. There will always be new curriculum to try, and a thousand different philosophies on teaching. Choose with what feels comfortable to you and fits your needs.

What if I am teaching multiple grades?

If I am researching one curriculum to be used with students at different levels, I try to pick one that is towards the mid-to-upper grade in my group. So for example if I have a preschooler, first grader, 3rd grader, and 4th grader, I will pick something around the 3rd grade level or something that is intentionally designed for multiple levels.

Curriculum Guide

To help narrow your search I have created a list of some of my favorite curricula for each subject. This is not an exhaustive list of curricula available, however is a guide that will help you get started in your researching process.

Note: You can find direct links for all of the resources listed on the following pages in the "resources" section at the back of this book.

Art	Bible
• Greatest Artists 1 • Greatest Artists 2 • Artistic Pursuits • How To Teach Art To Children • Deep Space Sparkle • Draw Write Now	• My Character Studies • Grape Vine Studies • What's in the Bible • Abeka • Answers For Kids
Handwriting	Health/ P.E.
• Abeka • A Reason for Handwriting • Handwriting without Tears • BJU Press	• Abeka • Family Time Fitness

Math	Music
• Math U See • Saxon • Teaching Textbooks	• Greatest Composers • Piano is Easy • Maestro Classics
Science	**Spelling**
• Scientists & Inventors • Apologia Science • God's Design • NaturExplorers • Abeka	• All About Spelling • Abeka • BJU Press
English/Grammar/Vocab.	**Foreign Language**
• Abeka • BJU Press • Easy Grammar • Rod & Staff English • Wordly Wise	• Rosetta Stone • PowerSpeak

History/Geography	Literature
• Expedition Earth World Geography • Road Trip USA • Abeka • Mystery of History • Time Travelers	• Classical Literature Units • Honey for a Child's Heart • Read for the Heart
Preschool	**Reading/Phonics**
• Letter of the Week • Before 5 in a Row	• Abeka • All About Reading • BJU Press • Explode the Code
Typing	**Writing**
• Typing Instructor • Typing Web	• WriteShop • Excellence in Writing

Chapter 3

Gathering Curriculum

Once you've decided on the curriculum for each subject you'll want to write them down on the "Our Curriculum" form (see Appendix). If you haven't already, complete this task for each subject, and each student.

Next, add prices next to each item so you can see what the cost is if you're buying new, as well as research prices online for used items whenever possible. Having a document with all of your prices comes in very handy when searching to purchase curriculum online or at a used curriculum fair.

Make sure to include what the current version of that curriculum is as well. This will also be helpful when searching for products.

Used curriculum fairs

My number one purchasing spot for used curriculum is at our annual used curriculum fair. I take my handy price sheet with me, so that I can easily decide if the cost of the used item is a good deal or not. It also helps in bartering with the seller. I typically purchase teacher's manuals for my oldest student at the used fairs as well as any other fun items that will benefit our homeschool. I HIGHLY recommend taking a list with you, as it's very easy to get overwhelmed with the amount of products found at a used fair. When buying used, make sure to determine if you can get associated workbooks for older versions of curriculum before purchasing.

State homeschool conventions

An online search should reveal any state homeschool conventions in your vicinity. Conventions typically include helpful seminars for homeschooling families as well as used and new curriculum sales. Talking to vendors and other homeschoolers can be very helpful in selecting your curriculum.

Bookstores

Most bookstores have a children's area that will include educational materials. This is a great place to see some of the materials in person; however prices are usually higher here. I typically examine potential materials here, but then order online for a better price.

Online purchasing

There are several online websites where you can purchase homeschool curriculum and books. Some of my favorites are Rainbow Resource Center and Christian Book. I've found many items at quite a discount compared to purchasing them new or at a fair. Of course major sites such as Amazon and eBay are always a good spot to check for pricing as well as reselling your own used items. Another great resource for used items is www.HomeschoolClassifieds.com where other homeschoolers buy and sell their used curriculum.

Buying new vs. used

I do my best to get anything for the upcoming year used if possible. I typically purchase all of the Teacher's Manuals for my oldest student, and then gather the consumables for the rest of the students. Since I will re-use those same Teacher's Manuals for my younger children when they are older, the only thing left to is gather workbooks and consumables that will have to be purchased new each year. So cost wise I'm really only making major curriculum purchases for one student each year. Think of it as homeschooling hand-me-downs.

I also make sure to keep track of the cost I end up paying for everything as I go, so that I have a record showing what I've spent on curriculum for each year. This will help in planning your budget for future years. Don't forget to add in those random purchases made throughout the year as well, so your cost assessment is accurate.

Keeping track of your costs will also come in handy if you ever decide to sell or trade your curriculum in the future.

Once each of your curriculum is acquired check off the box stating that you've actually obtained the curriculum so you don't accidentally repurchase!

Chapter 4

Homeschool Convention Tips

What's a Homeschool Convention you ask? Oh my! They're awesome, that's what they are! That's right! All of the amazing homeschool curriculum vendors meet up to display and share knowledge on all of their materials. There are usually workshops taught on various homeschooling topics by wonderful speakers to help you get started on your journey. And many even offer used sales areas for people to come and sell their used curriculum at a bargain rate! You know that's where I get most of my materials!

In this chapter we're talking about how to get through a homeschool convention in style!

Or at least with all your hair and sanity still intact.

Homeschool conventions

Here are a few of my favorite Homeschool Conventions. I can't say enough good things about the people who put on these conventions. They pick wonderfully inspiring speakers, and really go out of their way to create a great experience for both new and veteran homeschoolers! They're definitely worth attending.

Teach Them Diligently: Locations include Tennessee, South Carolina, Washington, D.C., and Texas.

Great Homeschool Conventions: Locations include South Carolina, Ohio, California, and Texas.

Not near any of these conventions?

Do a simple internet search for homeschool conventions in your state and see what's available to you! Or check out www.homeschoolconventions.com to see what's available as well!

Choosing a homeschool convention

To help you decide which homeschool convention is best for you and your family, here are a few ideas to take into consideration.

We like to keep close to home because it's less costly as far as travel expenses, and simply easier for us to attend. But there are a few other factors to take a look at when choosing which convention is best suited for your family.

Location

My top priority is location. I'm a busy mama of four and driving half way across the country isn't always feasible for our schedule. So for now I stick to conventions that are close by. Do a Google search to see what is near to you.

Speakers

Visit the website for the convention speakers and read up on their stance on homeschooling. Find those that best match your homeschooling needs at the time, or those that align with your overall homeschooling vision. You can use this to help you decide between two conventions.

Workshops

Each convention offers unique workshops to help address the needs of homeschoolers. Take a look at what is being offered and see which one fits your current needs the best.

Vendors

One great thing about homeschool conventions are the vendors. Not only do they show up with their physical curriculum, but they are also there to answer questions one on one and help you pick what is best for your family. I personally love leafing through physical curriculum as opposed to trying to look online. You can often get a much better feeling for how a curriculum will work if you can touch it and ask questions! Take a look and see which vendors you would most like to see and use that to help you decide which convention to attend.

Preparing for a convention

My number one purchasing spot is at our annual used curriculum fair. I take my handy price sheet with me, so that I can easily decide if the cost of the used item is a good deal or not. It also helps in bartering with the seller. I typically purchase teacher's manuals for my oldest student at the used fairs as well as any other fun items that will benefit our homeschool. I HIGHLY recommend taking a list with you, as it's very easy to get overwhelmed with the amount of products found at a used fair. When buying used, make sure to determine if you can get associated workbooks for older versions of curriculum before purchasing.

But if you're not prepared, homeschool conventions can be extremely overwhelming and nerve wracking!

Register in advance

Many homeschool conventions offer early bird registration. That's your chance to save a lot of money and make sure you get into the workshops of your choice. Pre-registering also helps the convention leaders know what to expect so they're better prepared to handle the amount of people headed their way. You can also avoid any long lines to get in the day of the event if you've already got your tickets in hand!

Plan ahead

Before attending your first or 15th homeschool fair, it's best to plan ahead. I normally research curriculum ahead of time so I know what I'm looking for. It's also a good idea to make a list of vendors you want to visit, and any questions you might want to ask them. Homeschool conventions can be very busy and overwhelming and there's a good chance you'll forget what you meant to ask!

I use my curriculum worksheet *(see Appendix)* to keep track of what I need to research or purchase. I also list new and used prices to make sure I get a good deal on curriculum.

Bring cash, checks, and credit cards

Many vendors will accept credit cards, however some smaller fairs, conventions, and used sales might only take cash or check so just be prepared.

Bring a backpack or small rolling suitcase

Yes a suitcase. I'll never forget the year I brought a small over the shoulder tote bag with me to our convention. Not only did I find GREAT bargains that year, but my bag was not nearly big enough to carry all of my newly found swag! My shoulder was killing me, and so were my book laden arms! Now I bring a carry on sized rolling suitcase. Since it rolls it's easy to manage and I don't have to lug it around on my back all day.

Go with a friend if you can

We team up as we're looking around the used fair. If one of us finds something we know a buddy is looking for we text them and hang on to it 'til the other person can get there. I know it sounds a little crazy, but if you can get your hands on your favorite curriculum for $5 it's worth it!

Give yourself plenty of time

Not only will there be a lot of great workshops to attend, but just browsing through all of the goodies can take some time. So don't think you can get through one of these babies in a couple hours. We usually take a day off and head up first thing in the morning. We eat lunch somewhere fun, and head back for any afternoon workshops.

Used sale tips

The early bird gets the worm people! Get there as soon as it opens if you plan to browse through the used sale arena. Curriculum sells fast, especially if deals are good!

Leave younger kiddos at home

Take this as my two cents, which is about all that it's worth. I don't bring my kids to curriculum fairs. I say this from the experience of bringing a newborn to my very first fair. It was cramped, crowded, loud, and crazy. Trying to get a stroller through the skinny halls full of people was just not ideal. I see many people with their whole families at fairs, and if that works for you awesome.

The only way I got through a fair with my baby was with the help of a BFF who also had her new baby there. We took turns standing at the end of the isle with the strollers while each of us went down the row one by one.

It was not fun. Nor was pushing a heavy stroller, and dealing with my sweet but overwhelmed baby, all while lugging around all of my purchases. I'm just sayin'. *(Rhonda, if you're reading this…I'll never forget that fair girl!)*

Get going

Now that you've chosen a convention, prepared, and are armed with knowledge, head out to your convention and enjoy learning all about the wonderful opportunities available for your homeschool this year.

Don't forget something to take notes on during the conference. You'll want to remember all of the great inspiration you receive there!

Oh, and you might consider bringing a pair of football pads and a helmet if you have them lying around… *Just kidding!*

Chapter 5

Creating Effective Lesson Plans

So now that you have your entire curriculum chosen and purchased, it's time to plan out your year. There are a couple schools of thought in this area. Some people choose to plan their lessons as they go, assuming that it will be easier to make changes as needed since they haven't planned too far ahead.

I personally like to plan out our entire year, even though there's a possibility something will change. It's been my experience that having my year completely planned out makes my year go more smoothly and reduces my amount of stress during the year as well. Changing just one thing is quite easily done.

Some people prefer to schedule only a few weeks or months in advance since things might change. Homeschooling schedules can be very flexible based on your own needs, so again, do what works best for the needs of your family.

This method also frees up your nights and weekends since all of the planning is already complete. All you have to do each Friday afternoon is make sure to have things ready for the upcoming week and then you have the rest of the weekend free to enjoy time with your family.

Curriculum → lesson plans

Now comes the fun part! It's time to transfer all of that shiny new curriculum into workable lesson plans to make your life easier. I know the thought of this can be overwhelming and frankly a daunting task. I won't claim to have the perfect solution for every family. However I will share how I organize our lessons into an ideal plan for our year.

Planning to plan

I know it might sound redundant to plan for your planning, but you will need something to keep you on track or you'll end up distracted by all that you need to accomplish. Taking the time to prepare ahead using the suggestions in this chapter, will greatly increase the effectiveness of your planning time.

I typically take a weekend to get all of my lesson planning done. Sometimes I don't get it all done that weekend and have to spend additional time to finish the lesson planning. The amount of time this step will take is going to depend on how old your students are and how many subjects you are planning for the year.

Prior to my "official" planning weekend, I make sure to take some time to go through each of my teacher's manuals for the upcoming year. Don't spend a ton of time on this step, just get a general feeling for how the manual is setup, and familiarize yourself with the curriculum. This will save time when you start to enter your lessons into your planner.

I also make a game plan of what I want to accomplish so I have a clue where to start. I like to start with one student, and plan one subject at a time. Then I move onto another, and finally another until I have gone through all of the subjects for that student. After that I will move onto the next student. For you it might make more sense to do one subject at a time for all of your students. You'll want to use whatever makes the most sense to you as your guide when planning.

So let's get started!

Determine school/holiday/vacation days

The first step in planning out your year is to decide what your year will look like. Taking into consideration your state requirements as well as any holidays, family vacations, etc., you'll want to create a basic outline for your year. You'll also want to decide if you prefer to follow a more traditional school schedule or homeschool year round taking breaks at times that work better for the needs of your family.

For this step I use an at-a-glance yearly calendar along with a blue, pink, and yellow highlighter. The yearly calendar will give you a nice overview of the year, and will help in deciding which days to schedule for school, holidays, and breaks. It will also help determine your start and end dates for the year. Of course you can do school year round, but it is still good for grades and record keeping selecting a start and ending date for each academic year.

I like the free yearly Blue Calendars from the Donna Young Website. They provide a clear calendar view for each school year. I have also provided printable year view calendars in the Appendix section of this book.

First, you'll want to figure out how many hours and days a week you need to account for based on your state homeschooling requirements.

If you haven't already checked, visit HSLDA for a listing for homeschool laws by state. For example, my state requires we complete an average of 4 hours per day over 172 days per year.

With my yearly calendar in front of me, I first go in and highlight any major holidays in blue. Once that is complete I highlight scheduled vacation days in pink. And finally I highlight our actual in-school days in yellow.

Keep this form handy so you can quickly transfer the information to your planning software or day planner as we proceed through our steps.

Planning Tip:

Plan "catch up days" into your schedule. Inevitably life gets crazy, kids get sick, and if you know you have every other Friday for catch up, you won't be so stressed when these things pop up unexpectedly.

Also, if you're homeschooling, you're never really behind, I mean you're the principal so you set the rules right?

Determine a basic schedule

Core subjects such as Math, Reading, and English are typically done each day, but this can be modified based on the needs of your family. Other subjects such as science, history, art, and music can be alternated weekly to fit your schedule.

During this step I take each of my subjects and look at the teacher's manual. Determine the number of lessons in the curriculum, and then divide the total number of lessons by the number of weeks you will be in school. This will help determine how many days per week you'll need to do that subject.

For example:

If your curriculum has 108 lessons in it, divide 108 by 36 weeks to learn that you must include this subject 3 times per week. You can then choose which days each week you want to complete that subject.

# of Lessons ÷ # of weeks = Lessons per week

Curriculum plan overview

Once your vacation days and school year are set, you can create a basic curriculum plan. Using the "Curriculum Plan Overview" form in the Appendix of this book, fill in formation for each subject as directed. Here you will note the total number of lessons, how many days per week you'll schedule this subject, an estimate of how much time will be spent on it, and what time of day you plan to do the subject. You can quickly refer to the teacher's manual for your curriculum to help fill in this information.

This form is the backbone to our upcoming step, which is adding the curriculum lessons into a planning software or day planner. Using your Curriculum Plan Overview, you will be able to quickly see how many lessons your subject encompasses, how many days per week you will need to schedule for this topic, how long a particular subject will take, and what time of day you plan to work on this subject.

Weekly overview

The next thing I like to do is quickly fill in a weekly overview based on my curriculum plan. The main reason I do this is so I can visually see if I've spread out my subjects well and that we haven't unintentionally overscheduled a day.

You can fill this form out a couple different ways. You can do a separate form for each student, or use color coded "X" to mark the subjects per student so you can quickly see what your week will look like with everyone included.

This form is a great place to add in extracurricular activities as well, so you can see how much you are realistically able to do per day. If you have too many "X"s on one day, rearrange the activities until you have a more realistic schedule.

Weekly Schedule Overview

Another great way to view your commitments is a weekly schedule overview. Here I write in subjects based on the times I've selected for each one. I also use a highlighter to color code each subject or activity so that I can quickly see at a glance what our day will look like.

Although you don't have to stick to this plan like glue, it is nice to have a basic daily schedule posted somewhere in your homeschool room so you can quickly see if you're staying on target each day. I've also noticed my children checking this form to see what they should be doing from time to time.

List extracurricular activities

Once my main schedule is set up, I then take the time to put in any extracurricular activities that we have agreed to do for the year. If you know that you will be doing something that takes place during the day, make sure to include that in your weekly schedule overview so you know not to schedule any subjects during that time.

Add the lessons into a planner

The next step in the planning process is to transfer all of your activities and lessons into a planning software, spreadsheet, or day planner. All of these items are acceptable means of planning, and really the format comes down to personal preference.

Here are a few of my favorite planners:

Planning Software:

- Homeschool Tracker for PC offers both free and paid versions of their software.
- Planbook for MAC offers a paid version of planning software.

Written Planners:

- My Lesson Planner – Floral
- My Lesson Planner – Colorful *(FREE - See Appendix)*
- Well Planned Day Planner
- Weekly Homeschool Planner

I prefer using electronic planning software because most will automatically keep track of hours, grades, and attendance. It is also easy to create several lessons at the touch of a button as opposed to handwriting each lesson which can be somewhat time consuming and difficult to adjust if your plan changes.

However I know several people who prefer the method of using a physical planner. Pick whichever method you prefer, and get ready to plan!

Add your predetermined school year, holidays, and days off into your planner

Since we already set these parameters in our previous steps, this should just be a matter of transferring the information from your calendar into the planner of your choice.

Note: If you are using an electronic planner and haven't already done so, you will need to add in your students, subjects, resources, etc. based on your planner's capabilities and how much data you want to store.

Add in your subjects into the planner

So let's get started with the logistics of adding lessons and activities into your planner.

Starting with one student and one core subject, open the teacher's manual for that subject. If you haven't done so already, quickly flip to the end to see how many total lessons there are and note that on your Curriculum Plan Overview form *(See Appendix)*. The teacher's manual should also tell you how much time you can expect to spend on each lesson. Make sure to note that on the Curriculum Plan Overview as well.

Open your planning software, or day planner, and enter the information for that subject into your planner. If you are using software you can most likely create all of the lessons at once, assigning the time, days, and hours for each one as you enter it.

If you are using something such as the Homeschool Tracker, I recommend adding in all of the lesson plans first, then going back through and assigning them out to the students that will be completing those lessons.

If you are using a day planner, handwrite the lessons into each day as indicated.

For either type of planner, you will probably want to include a brief set of instructions for each lesson to help you as you go through the year.

> For example I might enter something like this:
>
> Reading: "*Book Title*" pgs. 1-15

You probably don't want to waste too much time entering in a ton of detail unless it's needed. If there is more information that I need to refer to for that lesson then I will add that in the notes (see next page), but again it's totally up to your needs.

Science: Lesson 15 –
Bean Experiment: See TM

Obviously you can add as little or much information as you would like in your own plans. Continue to add in the lessons for your student one subject at a time. When finished with your oldest student, move to the next oldest, and so on until you have all of your lessons for core & elective subjects entered into your planner.

Plan crafts, field trips, & extra reading

As you go through the lessons more thoroughly you'll want to make note of any craft supplies, recipe ingredients, field trips, and extra reading that you would like to add in during your year. Make note of these things, and then use them as your guide when purchasing and planning anything needed for the year.

(You can find forms for all of these activities in the free download; see the Appendix for more information.)

A little bit of preparation can take a lot of stress out of homeschooling. Imagine running a race without knowing where the finish line is. If you've taken the time to plan ahead you'll already be familiar with what you're doing. You know where your finish line is which makes it easier to stay on task. You know when it's okay to take a day off here or there, and when it's not. You won't be unprepared for a craft or project, and you'll actually have more time to include fun stuff into your day. Then you can relax and enjoy the year!

Continue with this process…

You'll continue with this process going through all of the subjects for your first student. Then you'll move on to your second student with all of their subjects, and so on.

This process can take some time, but it will be well worth it once your school year starts. Planning ahead like this allows you to relax during the year, and follow your plan knowing that you'll be able to accomplish what you set forth to do.

Check your plans

Once your year is planned, print out the first couple weeks to visually make sure they look okay. You'll want to make any adjustments as needed to the plan at this time. If you've overscheduled something, or need to add in something now is a great time to do that as well.

Back up your plans

If you are using planning software, make sure to back up your files if possible so that all of your hard work isn't accidentally erased. If you are using an online program, find out what their policy is and if it is possible I highly recommend downloading a backup copy of your lesson plans.

Put your plans into action

Since homeschooling is a fluid beast, I don't recommend printing the entire year of lessons out all at once. Instead print one to two weeks of your lessons just to get you started. That way if you need to adjust times, curriculum, or tasks you can do so without having to waste a bunch of printed, and now inaccurate, lesson plans.

I typically print out my plans only one week at a time. I print them at the end of the week, for us that is usually Friday afternoon, so they're ready for the upcoming week.

I quickly glance over them to make sure there isn't anything I need to purchase or prepare for the week. Once I've skimmed the lessons I put them in an easily accessible location for the week.

Use your plan to quickly check off completed items as you progress through your day. At the end of the week, place your completed plan into your teacher's binder and print off a new one for the upcoming week.

Why print your plans?

Depending on your software, you should have a variety of reports you can print out. I prefer to print the ones that show an entire week's worth of assignments for each student, but you can choose whatever is available in your software. I then give a copy of that print-out to my older students so they can easily check off the items on their list. I keep the printout for my younger students so I can check off the items for them.

To mark an item complete, use a highlighter and highlight the lessons as they are finished. This helps keep you on task, as well as make sure you don't forget to do a particular assignment.

Once the week is over, add the highlighted lesson plan to a master binder for each year. To see more on how to organize and store your homeschooling items, see the next chapter of this book.

If you are using a day planner, you might consider making a copy of your planner, or getting a separate planner for your older students so they can see what they need to get done each day and mark them off as they go.

Rest!

Now that you've done your work, it's time to take a breather! Get out and enjoy a walk or spend time with the family doing something other than lesson planning!

When you're feeling refreshed, take a look at your plans, adjust anything necessary, and relax knowing you're ready to start your year.

How We Homeschool: To see a list of helpful links on our curriculum choices, our schoolroom setup, and our daily schedule visit www.confessionsofahomeschooler.com then click on "about us".

Chapter 6

Getting Organized

Organizing all of those fun school supplies is my favorite part of homeschooling. Preparing your school area is not only fun, but also a wonderful way to start the year. Kids will get excited about the prospect of a new year, and you as the teacher will rest comfortably knowing that your school area is organized and ready!

Prepare your school area

There are tons of different *ways* to homeschool, and with it are just as many *places* to homeschool. Some families do school in the kitchen, some at the library, and some outside if the weather allows. Some people even have a room or specific area of the home dedicated to homeschooling. Whatever the Lord has blessed you with; make the most of your space.

You can see a video tour of our homeschool room on my YouTube channel. *(Link in the "reference" section of this book.)*

Set it up in such a way that it makes sense to you, so things will be easy to find. Also try to make sure everything has a place to be stored so you don't have clutter hanging around on a regular basis. Having some order will help you find things during school, as well as make it easier to put things away after school. Making your space functional is important because as any veteran homeschooler will tell you, homeschooling can get a little crazy. And digging around in a pile of chaos during the middle of a lesson is not ideal.

So I am going to give you some basic tips on how we organize our homeschooling space that will hopefully help you get started. I will try to address as many areas as I can, but keep in mind some may or may not fit with the needs of your family. Please don't feel like you don't have the capability to homeschool just because you don't have a formal homeschooling area. There are many different options when setting up a homeschooling area.

Workspace

The first thing to consider is the workspace for your students. All homeschoolers will need an adequate space to work. This is especially important for younger students who are still learning how to write and need a more ergonomically correct environment.

When my children were first starting out, we purchased small individual desks for them which worked fine while they were younger. But as they got a bit older it became apparent that we really needed a bit more space to spread out books and supplies during lessons. We eventually settled on a larger communal type desk for everyone that allowed us more room to spread out.

Think about what your family's needs will be, and take into account the long haul so you don't waste money on something that won't be useful in a year or two. Keep in mind that your kitchen or dining room table works just as well, so don't feel like you have to go out and spend money on school desks in order to be successful at homeschooling.

Storage space

Oh beloved storage space! While it is possible to have a more minimalist approach to homeschooling, you will still need some type of storage for books, supplies, and student materials. Some people manage to store everything in the cabinets in their kitchen, some use drawers under counter tops. And others, like us, have an actual school room.

Whatever area you have designated for school, organized storage can be a very helpful tool. If things are stored in a functional manner it can remove a lot of stress and chaos from your day. Here are some guidelines to help you get started.

- Make supplies easily accessible.
- Store books and supplies in logical groupings. *(Keep like things with like things.)*
- Store items in kid friendly locations. *(i.e. don't put your preschooler's books on the top shelf.)*

I prefer the Ikea Expedit shelving units. They come in a variety of sizes and shapes to help accommodate your space. They are also sturdy and the shelf cubby holes are a great size for binders, and storing a lot of things. Of course you can use whatever is available to you, and fits your storage needs.

Teacher organization

I organize our shelves by topic, and also keep all of my teacher's manuals together by grade/student so they're easy to find. I also keep things that our children might need to access down lower so they're not climbing up the shelves to get something. Organize your materials however best makes sense for your space, and remember "keep like things together."

Teacher's Manuals

I keep all of my teacher's manuals in one place. You can sort them by grade or subject. I prefer to separate my teacher's manuals by grade level. When it's time to do a lesson for one of my students, I to go their shelf and pull out the manual for that subject. I have also seen people put all of their TM's in one binder with divider tabs so they're all on one spot.

Basic Supplies

Find a sensible area to store basic homeschool supplies. I keep most of our basic supplies in my desk area. For example I usually have glue, highlighters, sharpies, tape, stapler & staples, lined paper, grid paper, pencils, paper clips, scissors, calculators, Post It notes, etc., in my desk drawer.

Yearly records binder

Keep receipts, lesson plans, notice of intent to homeschool, and any other annual forms in a 1" 3-ring binder. Keep this binder easily accessible so you can add to it as needed during the year. At the end of the year, move that binder to your long term storage and start up a new one for the next year. Use divider tabs to keep things separated. Keep your binder in a handy location so you are more likely to put documents away on a regular basis. Inside the binder make tabs for the following information:

Legal Documents

Keep your annual "Notice of Intent to Homeschool" form or your enrollment in an umbrella school in this portion of the binder.

Receipts

Keep all receipts together for things you've bought for each school year. Most states don't allow a tax write off right now, but you never know! This is also good for budgeting purposes, and it also comes in handy for proving you homeschool when purchasing from companies that give educational discounts.

Lesson Plans

While this may or may not be required by your state, I like to keep a printed copy of our lesson plans for each student. I have dividers that separate out the lesson plans for each child to make it easy.

Once the year is over I bring my completed binder down and add it to a banker box containing my records from previous years. That box is stored on a shelving unit in our basement. That way these documents will be easily accessible and can be quickly located in the craziness that can take over a basement. Typically these binders contain documents that might be required by the state so I definitely want to keep these organized and easily accessible.

Student organization

Most of you know I've used some form of the workbox system developed by Sue Patrick for the past several years. I have to say that organizing our daily work has been a sanity saver for me. Put, the workbox system is a way to organize all of the daily school work for your student. You can use rolling carts, plastic crates, file folders, accordion files, or whatever else fits your needs.

See a workbox video tutorial on my YouTube Channel:

www.youtube.com/user/EricasHomeschool

Using this organizational system, you will keep everything needed for one subject into each drawer, file folder, or whatever organizer you choose. That way your student can easily see what they are to do each day. It helps students work independently as well as keeps everyone on track for the day. As the teacher you are responsible for re-filling the work each day so that it is ready to go.

Using this type of system has helped me stay organized during our hectic homeschooling day. This method also allows students to move through their work more independently. I can easily direct them to move on to another activity until I'm able to help them if needed. It also provides a visual for how much work they may have on any given day, how much they have accomplished, and how much left until they are finished. It's also easier for me to see if someone skipped something, or didn't do a lesson.

Completed School Work

I find it best to have an easily accessible location for completed work. I use stacking paper files for this. For example in our homeschool, as students complete their work, I have them put it on my desk for grading. Once the work is graded, I pass it back to students to correct. Finally, we place completed and corrected work into each student's file tray. I periodically clear out the tray and place the student work in a 3" 3-ring binder kept on my teacher's shelves. This just stores completed work until our year is over and I move it to the basement into long term storage.

Student Work Binders

I use 3" – 3 ring binders that we re-use for each child each year. It has dividers that separate each subject and I file our work in the binder as it's completed; i.e.: create divider tabs for Math, Language, Phonics, Spelling, Art *(I only keep stuff that fits)*, Science; Handwriting. The below binders are 3" binders, they store quite a bit of work. And I keep the current year's binders on our shelves in our homeschool room for easy access. As my files fill up, I put the completed work in these binders until the year ends.

Long Term Storage for Student Work

I like to keep bankers boxes in the basement for our long term storage. I keep one box per student, then band all of their work at the end of the year and place it in the banker box. This box is stored in our basement on shelving units.

Manipulatives

Store like things together. If you have younger students chances are you also have a ton of objects already that you can use for various activities. I try to store manipulatives together based on subject. For example store language/phonics things together, math things together, puzzles together, etc. Here are some ideas for storage:

- Small plastic containers (Take out side dish containers work well.)
- Plastic Ziploc baggies
- Rubbermaid Tupperware dishes

Books

As a homeschooling family you're bound to have quite a few books lying around! Here are a few tips to help keep them organized and easy to find.

Organize Books by Topic

Depending on your needs, I suggest storing books by topic. For example we store all of our holiday books together, and then separated by holiday for example: Christmas Books, Thanksgiving Books, Easter Books, etc. I also store them by subject as well.

Organize by Grade Level

You may also choose to store your readers by grade level. This makes it easier for your students to pick out a book that is appropriate for their age or reading level. Often we will mark them with a colored dot sticker to note which books go with what grade.

Technology

Most homeschools include some sort of technology. I have all of our 'electronic' items in one area. We keep a computer used for online education as well as our iPad on my desk. If possible make it so this area is ergonomically efficient for the ages of your students. Keeping electronics in one area helps you keep track of everything, and helps you to monitor its usage.

Wall space

As a homeschooler, wall space is your friend! Use it wisely and it will serve your family well.

Posters & Other Visuals

Keep visuals low enough for kids to see them easily. Having an alphabet strip up at the top of the room for a preschooler isn't exactly effective. Use posters and other things relevant to what you are teaching, this will most likely change from year to year.

Whiteboards

Most people will need some type of writing surface in their homeschool room. I recommend either a white board, or chalk board for this need. We use our whiteboard for almost everything. I also suggest getting one large enough to fit more information than you think you will need. We currently have a 5 ft. x 8 ft. white board which is almost always completely full of information on any given day.

Keep it useful

Wall space is precious! Keep your wall space fun and colorful, but make sure that the materials are also useful. Some ideas include creating a daily calendar time area, topical posters, maps, sight words, timelines, an alphabet strip, and a cork board to display completed student work.

Long term storage space

Another aspect of storage is the long term storage. First, you will want to check the homeschooling laws for your state to see what you are required to keep. Next, be prepared to keep everything regardless of your state laws because after all of that hard work, you can't bear to part with it.

We store all previous years' work and curriculum not currently in use in our basement. There is a shelving unit specifically for school related items only.

Student work: Long term storage

The records you are required to keep will be determined by your state requirements. Most states do not make you keep everything for each year. However, many will request an attendance sheet showing hours and days completed for each student. Some states will also require a list of curriculum used each year as well. Find out what your state laws are before you delve into the practice of storing all of your student's work. You'll find that it adds up quickly and many of us don't have the storage space required to keep all of everything over the years.

For the time being, I have chosen to keep our work for my own fond memories. I also have a hard time throwing out a full year's worth of sweat and tears! So for now, I have purchased banker's boxes to store my students' completed work in.

At the end of each year, I remove all of the paper, artwork, and anything else they've done and bind it together using a rubber band, or string. I put a strip of paper on the front of the bundle indicating the student's name, year, and grade level of the bundle. Then place that bundle in the banker's box for that student. Each student has their own box full of work from previous years. The boxes are clearly labeled with their name, and what years of work it contains.

Curriculum: Long term storage

I use banker's boxes to store any curriculum that isn't currently in use. For us this is mainly curriculum we will use in the future and I'm not ready to sell yet. I label the boxes by subject. So for example I have a "Math" box that contains our math curriculum in grade order. Since we do some subjects together, and some individually based on grade, having them separated by subject makes it makes it easier for me to see what I have.

For example our math curriculum box *(above)* has the curriculum we use for math for Kindergarten through our current grade (or however many years will fit!). Keeping the boxes sorted by Curriculum allows me to easily grab the grade level as needed or see that we don't have that grade level and I can then order it for our upcoming year.

Some people might prefer to box their curriculum by grade. You are free to use whatever organization makes the most sense to you. I have found that organizing my curriculum helps greatly when planning for an upcoming year. It's easy for me to see what I have and what I will need to purchase for that year. It also keeps me from purchasing duplicates of something because I couldn't locate it. Organizing your curriculum is also helpful when getting ready to sell old materials as well.

School supplies

I must admit I'm a total school supply junkie! I love everything about new school supplies, love to shop for them, love to organize them when we get home, and love to pull them out on day one!

As a homeschooler we have the freedom to purchase whatever we need, we don't have to go off of a required list. And we are also buying supplies for our own children to use in our own homes. This makes shopping a little more fun. We can purchase colorful things, let students pick out what they like, and know that the supplies we're purchasing will go to good use.

Here is a list of some of the supplies we purchase almost every year to help you get started. Wherever possible I let my children pick the things that they like so they're also excited to start school.

You can find a more detailed list of homeschool supplies & organization on my website.

You will also find a School Supply Shopping List in the free homeschooling forms that come with this book. See the Appendix for information on to access these forms.

School clothes

One thing I always loved about a new year, was shopping for new school clothes. Since our family homeschools this isn't really a necessity, but I still don't want my children to miss out on it. So we will usually do some of our shopping for the next season at this time.

Normally I purchase new or used clothing for our oldest, and then pass her clothes down to the others. For our younger children, I will clean out their closet at this time and re-fill it with the "new-to- them" clothing from their older sibling. They still get excited about having a new selection of outfits to wear.

We also purchase shoes for them at this time as well. For our family each child gets a new pair of tennis shoes and then a fun pair or dress pair depending on our needs at that time.

Chapter 7

Starting School - Day 1

Once your curriculum is ordered, lessons are planned, the work area is organized and ready, it's time to start school! Typically students and teachers are excited for the first day and it's no different in your homeschool.

To help foster our excitement I let students help to set up the school room, purchase supplies, and organize their work area. Once it's officially time to start school, everyone is excited and ready to go!

Some people like to start school on a Wednesday, so they're only doing three days the first week, then break for the weekend, and then start in on Monday with a full week of lessons. I typically start on Monday, but keep the first day light and fun.

Remember, there is not one "right" way to homeschool, and what works for one student might not work for another. What works for one family might not fit for another. So keep in mind God's ideal for your family, and choose what fits best for you. Don't waste time comparing your homeschool to others, because no two look the same.

The night before our first day I like to do a special end of summer dinner. We usually have a fun outside BBQ with a special dessert. Then we make sure that everyone gets to bed at a decent hour so they're well rested.

Day 1

On the first day of school, I usually plan to cook a special breakfast so I know that our children are ready to learn! If needed, remind them to get a drink and use the bathroom prior to starting. There's nothing like starting on day one and having everyone ask to use the bathroom right off the bat!

Next, we head outside to take first day pictures. As a homeschooler this is something we can forget to do, but it's a great way to commemorate the day, so don't forget to take pictures!

Next, we do a quick tour of our new school area and make sure everyone knows where things are located. Then I let the children take a few minutes to go through their workboxes to see what is in store for them this year. We also take a moment to review our rules so everyone is familiar with them.

Next we discuss our pre-determined daily schedule so everyone knows what will be expected of them through the day. As we progress through the first few days, I also remind them as we are going what we have next so they become familiar with the schedule.

Finally we start our day with the Pledge of Allegiance, then move on to our lessons.

Since it's your first day, try to keep it light. Allow students time to get used to the new schedule, and if you're a new homeschooler, they'll need time to get used to homeschooling itself.

Don't be discouraged if day 1 is harder than expected. Or if day 1 is fabulous, but day 2 or 3 things start to fizzle. There is an ever-so slight chance your student's excitement may fade once they learn that school is hard work. I encourage you to keep a positive attitude, and if necessary gently remind students of your rules as well as rewards for good behavior.

What should my daily schedule look like?

I've had numerous questions on what our daily schedule looks like. While each day can bring on a life of its own, we do have a basic schedule or more of a routine if you will. Barring any unforeseen circumstances we do our best to stick to this routine. I find that both my children and I do better with a general overall guideline of how their day will go.

While everyone's routine will vary, I know as a new homeschooler just having an example to start off with is helpful. So for what it's worth, here is what our typical daily schedule looks like. Keep in mind the schedule in a homeschooling home is a fluid thing and can change.

You know …provided nothing unexpected happens…like say my toddler decides to paint the floor with her new blue fingernail polish.

Our schedule

7:30 am – Mom Showers/get dressed

8:00 am – Breakfast, start a load of laundry *(I usually do 1 load per day, sometimes 2)*

8:30 am – SCHOOL STARTS

- 8:30 – Bible
- 9:00 – Math
- 9:30 – Spelling
- 9:45 – Handwriting
- 10:00 – English/Snack
- 10:30 – Reading
- 11:00 – Free Reading Time (Kids can pick any book they want, but must read for 15 min.)
- 11:15ish – LUNCH BREAK (Switch out laundry to dryer)
- 12:15 – History/Science (Alternate doing each 2x per week)
- 12:45 – Piano/Typing (Alternate doing each 2x per week)
- 1:00 – World's Greatest Composers/ART (Alternate doing each 1x per week)
- 1:30 – Writing
- 2:00 – Classic Literature Units

2:30 pm – SCHOOL ENDS *(Well you know, technically it ends…realistically my kids are subject to my constant pop quizzes all day long.)* Once school is done, I re-fill workboxes while the kiddos clean up their areas and make sure the school room is all nice and pretty like it was when we started so we are ready for the next day.

3:00 pm – Chore time: Everyone does what they can from their chore chart assignments. Fold and put away laundry, dishwasher, etc.

3:30 pm – Free Time *(Kids play while I check email, etc.)*

5:00 pm – Dinner Prep *(Kids set table and some help me prepare dinner…depending on their mood of course…and mine!)*

5:45pm: 10 Minute Tidy: This is where I set a timer and everyone runs around like maniacs cleaning up anything can they find so when Daddy comes home the house is a clean and serene oasis so he assumes it's like that all day *…sorry honey, the secret is out…please don't come home any earlier than 5:50 unannounced or my reputation will be ruined forever.*

6:00pm: Dad enters & asks *"So, what did you do all day?"* I say *"Not much, just lounged around and ate bon-bons."* Dad quizzes kids to make sure I'm kidding.

6:00ish – Dinner/dishes/sweep kitchen floor *(Seriously, how does it get destroyed after 1 meal?) This may also be a sport night in which* *case dinner is pushed up some and we attend our various extra-curricular activities.*

7:30pm – Family devotions & bedtime (Clean up rooms, take baths, brush teeth, go to bed!)

8:30pm: Free time for mom and dad....sit down for first time today and sigh… and praise God we made it through another homeschool day without burning down the house!

That is our basic daily schedule in a nutshell. Obviously we don't follow this down to the minute; however we do tend to keep the same basic format to our days barring unforeseen circumstances. Our children know what to expect on most days, and so our homeschool time has just naturally become part of our week.

I'd also like to encourage you to defer from emailing, making and receiving phone calls, as well as any other random activities that might take you from your school time. Make your best effort to be physically and mentally available to your students during school.

There are moments where my attention may be diverted, but I do my best to stay available for my children during our school hours. We cannot expect our students to be diligent with school work, if we are not also assiduous in our duties as their teacher.

How long should school take?

A full school day currently takes us about 4 hours for the older kids (3rd & 4th grades), about 3 hours for my 1st grader, and about an hour to an hour and a half for my preschooler. However, you will want to check with your state for hourly attendance requirements.

Preschool

On an average day I usually spend 1-2 hours for a preschooler per day depending on what they can handle. If your preschooler starts to get frustrated or disinterested let them take a break and either return to activities later in the afternoon, or the next day. Keep in mind that most preschoolers attend school only 2-3 half-days per week, so there is no need to force a certain amount of time.

Kindergarten

For us, Kindergarten usually takes about 2-3 hours per day to complete all of our work. Each subject only takes about 15-20 minutes depending on their attention span. Again you'll want to check your state requirements.

Elementary and beyond

From first grade and up most states will require a certain amount of attendance averaging a specific amount of hours over the course of your year. You will need to consult your state's requirements to see how much time you should be spending on school each day.

Most curricula will give you a guideline for the appropriate amount of time to spend on that subject. It might also be based on age. This will help you when planning out your day.

Chapter 8

Homeschooling Multiple Grades

Depending on your homeschooling family, you may find yourself needing to teach more than one grade level simultaneously. While this may seem like an overwhelming situation, with a little preparation and patience you can successfully teach multiple grades. Here are some tips to teaching multiple grade levels at the same time.

Group work

I suggest that you try to do as much together as possible to save time and make teaching easier. We typically like to do our group work first thing in the morning. Then once our group subjects are completed we move into our more independent work. This helps eliminate students waiting for others to complete work so they can do something as a group. It also lets students move at a more independent pace once group subjects are complete.

We work on our Daily Learning Notebooks, Bible, Science, History, Literature, Art, and Music as a group. For the most part this works for more elective type subjects. We also do Calendar Time together for the younger students. Then move onto independent grade levels for core subjects such as math, English, reading, and spelling.

The balancing act

After the group work is completed, we move onto our individual work. We still tend to do like subjects at the same time however students will move at their own speed once you hit this step. For example, we do math at the same time even though I have 3 students working on different levels. I start off having my oldest watch her Math U See video, and then she moves onto her worksheets, while the next student watches their video. I have another computer at home, so my 3rd student uses that and then moves right to her worksheet. As all the students are working on math, I stand by and supervise or help as needed.

We basically follow the same format for the other subjects alternating my teaching one student at a time. For example, I will teach an English lesson together with the older two. While they're working independently on the accompanying worksheet, I will do a phonics lesson with my 1st grader. So it will look something like this:

- Teach lesson to student 1 → Student 1 does independent work associated with lesson taught.
- Teach lesson to student 2 → Student 2 does independent work associated with lesson taught.
- Teach lesson to student 3 → Student 3 does independent work associated with lesson taught.

Repeat this process with remaining lessons as needed…

As you can see I teach a lesson to one of the students, then while they're working independently I move to the next student, and so on. Our day progresses like this as we go, alternating between me teaching and them working.

You will get more used to alternating between students as each year progresses. The kids will also learn to work a little more independently as well.

Independent work

Another key to working with multiple grade levels at the same time is to have a few subjects that are more student independent in nature. While we do not use all online or DVD type classes, I do suggest creating a nice balance between teacher led and student independent courses.

If you run into a situation where more than one student is ready for a lesson at the same time, you can easily divert a student to one of their independent activities until you are available.

To pick which subjects you want to be more student independent, choose which subjects you're comfortable teaching, and then look into alternatives for the others. We like to utilize online courses and DVD courses.

So for example, currently our independent subjects are handwriting, typing, and math.

- Handwriting is fairly easy to follow so unless my student needs help forming a certain letter, they can do that independently.
- For typing we use a DVD program called Typing Instructor. This program does not typically require assistance from me to complete. It keeps track of the

student's progress, and keeps a records page so I can make sure they are working diligently. There are also online typing programs as well, see chapter 2 of this book for curriculum suggestions.

- Currently we are using the Math U See program. This comes with a video lesson on DVD, and then students work on mastering the skills for that lesson over the course of the week. Since the lesson is taught on the DVD, I only need to be available to help students as needed during the week. This frees up some of my time to work with other students while one is viewing their DVD lesson.

If you have multiple students, I highly encourage you to choose at least a couple 'go-to' student independent subjects. Choosing curriculum that is highly teacher intensive will be difficult to manage in a multiple level homeschool situation.

Chapter 9

Homeschooling & Discipline

As the excitement of starting school wears off, you may begin to notice some disobedience starting to creep in. I would love to say that our children are perfectly obedient all the time, but that just isn't true. So we did have to put some basic discipline tactics in place. My main goal is to keep everyone focused on their work rather than disturbing those around them. Since we do most subjects together it can be a problem if someone isn't working diligently or distracting others.

In our home, if kids aren't paying attention, or choosing to mess around when they should be working, they are required to put their unfinished work in a 'homework' pile to be completed at the end of the day. That way their poor choices aren't affecting the rest of us. Then we can all move on to our next subject and stay on schedule. My children have learned quickly that it pays to get your work done without dawdling! Honestly, they don't do that too many times before they realize it's no fun to be doing school work when the other siblings are off playing.

In a homeschool setting it can be difficult for some students to stay focused. Most students will naturally learn to tune out their younger siblings while working, however some might need some assistance in this area. It was very difficult for Turbo to start off, so I used to give him a pair of my husband's shooting ear muffs to block out the noise. *I wrote about it in a post called "Ear Protection for Peace".* You may also consider putting up folding cardboard pieces around their area, or allowing them to do school in a quieter part of your home, if age appropriate.

I also make sure that I'm doing my job by being present in our homeschool area, available for questions, or keeping people on task. If needed, I gently remind them to be respectful of those working around them.

Rewarding positive behavior

The best way to help curb whining is to reward positive attitudes and those who are working hard. Putting up a sticker chart and rewarding students with a sticker for each day that they chose to work diligently is a great way to motivate students to do their best. Once their sticker chart is filled up, allow them to pick some sort of reward.

Some ideas include a gift from a small prize box, a special treat for dinner, maybe a trip to get ice cream, or whatever makes sense for your family.

Whining and complaining

Most whining and complaining fades as students get more used to homeschooling and what is required of them. When we started out, there was quite a bit of whining...

"How much more work is there?"

"Can I be done now?"

"Why do I have to work while my sibling is playing?"

"I don't feel like doing that!"

The workbox system I've mentioned really helps out in the area of whining and complaining. When students can visually "see" their work for the day, there's no question of how much work there is, how much is left, or when they can be done. Organizing your students work can go a long way in reducing the amount of complaining you'll receive.

In addition to the workboxes, we made a rule that whining in class would not be tolerated. There are a few ways to handle this. You can implement something similar to what schools do and put student's initials up on your white board, and then give them a check for each time they complain. If they hit 3 checks, then they get to have a personal meeting with the principals (Dad and Mom) to explain why they made bad choices during the day.

You can make a wall chart with 'green, yellow, red' cards in them. If they're having a green day they are doing well, yellow means they've received a warning regarding their choices that day, and red means they have a meeting with the principals to explain their behavior and receive appropriate consequences for their actions.

In our home, students also meet with mom and dad at the end of the day if they had to stay after to do homework, to explain why they were messing around instead of doing their work diligently. They may also lose a privilege, such as a play date, depending on their choices that day.

Chapter 10

Standardized Testing

As with everything, you'll want to start by checking your state requirements to determine if standardized testing is required. Some states offer testing or yearly assessments which are less stressful for the student, so it is good to know what your requirements are.

I prefer to test regardless of my state requirements because I use the tests to gauge how well my students are doing. We choose to test annually starting in 2nd grade. In my state testing is required starting in 3rd grades and every odd grade after that. I begin in 2nd grade to give my students a "trial run" test. This allows them to get used to the test itself as well as lets me know if there is an area we need to work on. You're welcome to do whatever works best for your family, or whatever is required by your state.

I know that standardized testing can seem daunting, but I want to assure you that it is not as difficult as you may think it is. The tests are fairly easy to order, administer, and submit. Our kids did very well on them and it was a nice re-assurance to me that we are doing well in our curriculum choices and decision to homeschool. We also have a few areas to work on, and that is a good thing to find out too.

Homeschool testing requirements vary by state, so you'll want to check recent laws by state, you can find information at the HSLDA Website. *PLEASE NOTE: I do not live in IOWA, the Iowa Standardized tests are available no matter where you live, you can administer any test you like as long as it is acceptable through your state requirements.*

I was previously nervous about the whole "testing" topic and had kind of avoided it, but really it was very easy. I wanted to share a little info with you all to relieve any test anxiety you may have as well.

Choose your tests

Per state requirements decide whether or not you will test your students each year. We choose to test annually starting in 2nd grade even though it is not required by our state. Stating in 2nd grade gives the student a "practice" year to get used to taking the tests. It also shows you as the teacher areas you may need to work on.

There are several different tests you can choose depending on your state requirements. Examples include the Stanford Tests, Iowa Test of Basic Skills, and California Achievement Tests.

I order the Stanford Tests or Iowa Standard Tests from BJU Press Testing. You can find more information on testing options at HSLDA Website.) If you are going to do Iowa Standard testing you will need to be approved as a test administrator prior to starting. There is a Test Administrator Application link on the sidebar of their website.

For the Iowa's, you will need to send in a copy of your Bachelor's diploma prior to being approved as a test administrator. I faxed over a copy of my degree and received approval within about 10 days. Pay attention to the testing requirements, some tests must be completed and returned within a certain time frame; your testing company will give you specifics when you order. I do not believe a bachelor degree is required to administer the CAT (California Achievement Tests) so that might be an option if you do not hold a degree.

If you do not have your Bachelor's degree, but still want to use the Iowa tests, you will need to find a certified testing administrator in your area.

You can contact BJU Press for help finding registered test administrators. Also make sure to check with local homeschool organizations. They often offer group testing and discounts. In addition many umbrella schools offer testing services even if you are not registered with them.

> **Tip #1 from the trenches:**
>
> If you know you are going to test this year, be proactive and set a date to order tests so they arrive close to when you finish school for the year.
>
> Students tend to "forget things" once they go into summer brain mode.
>
> Test in the final quarter of your year, that way students haven't checked out for the summer yet, and you have had a chance to teach most of the new skill sets for the year.

Optional Practice Tests

If you just want an evaluation for the year, or if you want to practice, you can order practice tests from BJU Press as well. They are less expensive and still give a good level of practice for teacher and student.

Administer the tests

Read the rules for administering your test. Depending on the grade you are testing you may be required to test certain grades separately.

You'll want to pick a well-lit spot, and provide a quiet time with little distraction. Your test will come with a suggested schedule, and for the most part we follow that. If you follow the test schedule in your book you'll see it can take up to a week to complete the tests if you do 2-3 per day. I found my kids did

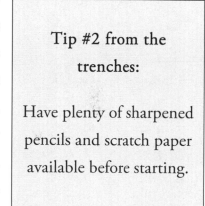

Tip #2 from the trenches:

Have plenty of sharpened pencils and scratch paper available before starting.

better when we did a couple per day as opposed to doing them all in one day, but you could certainly choose to do that. We had "Testing Week" at our house and at the end of the week we took everyone out for ice cream to celebrate.

Send in your completed tests

You'll want to follow all return directions for whatever tests you purchased. Flip through your test booklets and make sure there are no stray marks or incomplete dots filled in so as not to skew your results. Make sure all items to be included are sent back or your results will not be processed.

The Iowa test will require you use a service such as FedEx or UPS so the package is traceable, so just make sure that you follow the rules listed on your test.

File your results

If it is a required testing year for you, you'll want to submit your test scores to the appropriate location. You will need to find out what is required in your state. In ours, I am required to submit my testing results on odd years starting at the end of grade 3 to my local school district, or I can also submit them to my umbrella school.

In some cases if you are enrolled in a public school funded options program (a.k.a. "Friday School" and the like) you are required to keep records of testing yourself. Either way, you'll need to find the appropriate method of submitting results for your state and follow those rules.

For more information on testing options and your state laws visit www.hslda.org.

Chapter 11

Homeschooling with Toddlers

Homeschooling with babies and toddlers in toe is a common occurrence for homeschoolers. And while it can be slightly daunting trying to teach math while nursing a baby, and trying to occupy a busy toddler, I can assure you it can be done.

As mentioned previously, flexibility is a key point in homeschooling. Depending on the year, school might need to be arranged to fit the needs of the younger ones in your home. Here are some tips and tricks to homeschooling with little ones in your midst.

Include your toddler

I know it might sound crazy, but my number one tip to homeschooling with toddlers is to include them in your lessons whenever possible. Even if that means giving them a blank sheet of paper or an old workbook and letting them 'work' with the older ones. Not only does it make them feel like they're part of the group, but it also occupies their time as well. I've found that trying to keep younger children separate is actually more distracting to everyone. If you can't see them you're worrying about what they're into, and rightly so. And if they feel they are not being included, they can tend to act out to get attention.

Take a look at what you are teaching your older students and then look for something related you can do with your younger ones. For example if you are doing math, bring out some counting bears for your toddler. Have them sort the bears by color, or count them together. If you are doing an art project, give them an apron and their own supplies and let them join in!

Make school time special

Make a box or set of activities that they are only allowed to play with during school time. Consider the concept of "preschool in a bag" type activities to keep them busy during school time. Whenever necessary bring out their own "special" work for them.

Here are a few suggestions that you can include in your toddler's activity box. For even more ideas on what to include visit my website and click on "Homeschool" and then "Tot School". *As always, parental supervision should accompany any activity that may pose a choking hazard.*

- Sorting objects (By color, size, texture, theme, etc.)
- Stacking objects (Stacking blocks, cups, etc.)
- Blocks (foam or wooden)
- Lacing large buttons, or blocks
- Play-Doh
- Play food & kitchen
- Role Playing
- Songs
- Read to your toddler. Board books and texture type books are great too!
- Magnetic Wooden Color Cubes

- Transferring objects with toaster tongs (pom-poms, balls, beads, etc.)
- Do-A-Dot Worksheets (Visit my printables page for a free copy!)
- Rush Hour Jr.
- Sorting Bears
- Pattern block cards and blocks by Learning Resources
- Letter Construction Activity from Learning Resources
- Parents Bristle Blocks
- Jumbo Dice in Dice
- Educational Insights Hot Dots Jr.
- Water color painting
- Guidecraft Nesting Sort & Stack Cubes
- Stickers and paper
- Number Sticker sheets
- Geoboards and Rubber Bands
- Zoob Builders
- Wooden Puzzles
- Cutting and pasting
- Coloring
- Melissa & Doug See & Spell
- Fisher-Price Trio building blocks
- Turkey buttoning activity

- Magnetic Match Rings
- Toot and Otto
- Holgate Toys Geo Lacing Shapes
- Unifix Sudoku and Unifix Cubes
- Peg Number Boards from Lakeshore Learning
- Wooden Lacing Beads & Pattern Cards
- Large Bag Clips and wooden color disks
- Numbers Puzzles
- Counting Keys by Lakeshore Learning
- Pattern Blocks and activity cards
- Great Big Buttons and Shoe Laces
- Solid Wood Teaser games
- Styrofoam block, golf tees, marbles (Have child push tees into foam, and then balance the marbles on top.)

Spend time with your toddler

As I mentioned previously, most toddlers are interested in spending time with you. If you have a small break between helping older students, or while they are working independently, make sure to spend some one-on-one time with your toddler. Read a quick book to them, or play a game with them. A small amount of attention in between helping older students will go a long way towards keeping your toddlers happy.

Another idea is to utilize your older students. For example, while you are teaching one of your other students, have an older sibling play a fun game with your toddler. Once you're done teaching, they can go back to their work and you can take turns playing with the younger student.

Give your toddler their own work space

I know it sounds premature, but offing a special work area for your toddler helps give them a sense of importance and belonging. Just like the older students have a work area. If they feel like they have their own special work area, they're much more likely to want to use it during school just like their older siblings.

Utilize electronic tools

We make good use of the iPad in our homeschooling. There are tons of preschool and toddler level apps out there to help not only occupy your toddler, but educate them at the same time. Visit my website to see a list of Educational iPad Apps.

Another one of my secret tools when nothing else seems to be working are the LeapFrog DVDs. <u>The Letter Factory</u>, <u>Talking Words Factory</u>, <u>Numberland</u>, <u>Adventures in Shapeville</u>, and <u>Math Circus</u> are just a few in the LeapFrog arsenal of great educational DVDs.

Use naptime wisely

The last tip for homeschooling with babies and toddlers is to use naptime as wisely as you can. There were many years where we did our core subjects during afternoon or morning naptime. Some subjects require more of your attention and students need to be able to concentrate. Having a busy toddler distracting everyone might not go over so well. Rearranging your schedule so you are working on those subjects during naptime can alleviate a lot of stress in your day.

Keep your babies close

If you are homeschooling with a newborn, or expecting one shortly, make sure to plan ahead. Remember that this is just a season, and it will pass quickly. You won't ruin your children by keeping things simple during this time.

Plan to keep your newborn close by. If possible, setup a pack-n-play in your homeschooling area, or somewhere near so it is easy to get to your baby's necessities quickly. I also recommend using a sling or some type of carrier for your newborns as well. This allows for ease of nursing while teaching. It's also nice to be able to comfort your baby when needed while still having your hands free to help your other students.

With a baby area set up close by, you can lay them down for a nap, change them, and feed them all without leaving your other students for too long. And we all know what happens when the teacher steps out of the class room!

If you're expecting a new baby I also suggest that you keep your school schedule to the basics. Don't feel like you have to do every subject every day. If your new baby needs you at an inconvenient time in the school day, have students work independently for a few minutes, or have them take a small reading break while you attend to your infant.

Another tip is to plan harder subjects during your babies sleep time. While your infant is resting, you will be able to focus more directly on the needs of your other children.

Having a new baby is wonderful, but can also be very tiring. Over planning, and trying to do everything as if nothing has changed isn't realistic. Plan to take a break when you have your baby no matter what time of year it is. Use this time to let everyone acclimate to the new addition and enjoy the time with your new baby while it lasts!

Chapter 12

Homeschooling Your Preschooler

Homeschooling a preschooler is probably one of the most exciting times. They're excited to learn, and keeping school fun at this age is a must! While there aren't any specific curriculum requirements for preschool, I encourage you to focus on creating a love of learning and keep your curriculum to the basics.

Preschool is the perfect time to start because you and your child will have the opportunity to grow and learn together. In essence, preschool is a very forgiving year. It's a time to try new things, enjoy time with your child, create fun art, make mistakes, change the way you do things, get a schedule figured out, and in a nutshell get acclimated to homeschooling. I like to use the preschool year to help students get used to a little more formal schedule without the pressure of having to do a certain amount of hours or days. It's a nice transitional year from free toddler playtime to more structured homeschooling.

If you've already been homeschooling for a while, it's your younger child's chance to get involved and have their own special school work. Preschool typically starts for children around age 3 to 4 years of age. But some students may be ready a little sooner, some a little later. Let your child help guide your decision of when to start based on their readiness.

You don't need some expensive curriculum; you can even plan the whole year on your own by gathering resources you'd like your child to learn. Most states don't have any requirements in regards to preschool level students. So there's really no pressure at all to do something specific, or to do anything structured at that age. It's totally up to you and what your child is ready for.

Keeping things fun will go a long way towards getting your preschooler ready for more formal homeschooling. Let your child help guide their day. You may find it necessary to gently encourage reluctant students to try something new. If you notice your preschooler getting tired, frustrated or bored with what you are doing, stop the activities and try again later.

That said I know for a new homeschooler leaving everything up in the air isn't very helpful, so I wanted to compile a list of things to help guide you in homeschooling your preschooler. Like I said, these are certainly not requirements, but will hopefully help you get started in planning your preschool year.

Don't feel as if you have to include every single thing listed on the following pages. However feel free to use the ideas that make the most sense for your student's skill level, and the goals for your homeschool. Just use this time to create a love of learning and help encourage your preschooler to explore the world around them.

> "Use this time to create a love of learning and help encourage your preschooler to explore the world around them."

Social skills

Preschool is mainly a time to prepare your child for the maturity needed to succeed in future school years. Much of it is learning to follow rules, be respectful of others, and learn some self-control skills.

Here is a small list of things that can be enforced during the preschool year.

- Help them gain self-confidence by doing things on their own
- Learn to Work more independently
- Teach them how to take care of supplies & belongings
- Teach them to learn how to follow rules
- Use good manners
- Display self-control
- Listen quietly when others speak
- Learn to share and respect others

Fine-motor skills

The other major part of preschool is honing in on fine-motor skills necessary for future schooling. Fine motor skills play a large part in the handwriting process and thus very important in preparation for kindergarten. Here is a small list of fine-motor skill type activities you can do with your preschooler to help build the necessary muscles.

- Holds crayons/pencils/markers correctly
- Scissor skills
- Cut and paste skills
- Assemble basic puzzle

- Copy a pattern
- Coloring pictures
- Buttoning
- Zipping
- Tying
- Snapping
- Lacing
- Play-Doh
- Transferring objects from one container to another using toaster tongs.
- Sticking small pixie straws into a container with small holes on top.
- Stick golf tees into a block of Styrofoam, and then have preschooler balance marbles on top of each one.
- Balance small glass beads or buttons on a large Popsicle stick.

Reading readiness

Another thing that is a good idea to cover is basic reading readiness skills. This does not only refer to letter recognition, but also left to right progression in reading, as well as stories, poems, and rhymes. Here is a list of some reading readiness activities you can cover.

- Using good sentences to communicate
- Using their imagination
- Parent read stories, poems, and rhymes
- Letter recognition Uppercase *(Includes learning sounds associated with the letters.)*
- Letter recognition Lowercase *(Includes learning sounds associated with the letters.)*
- Identifying words that rhyme
- Tracing their name
- Tracing or writing letters
- Basic understanding of left to right progression *(A good way to reinforce this skill is by using your finger and pointing to the words as you are reading them. Also point to numbers on a calendar as you count going from left to right, then back down to the next row and across again.)*

Verbal skills

Verbal skills are something that will naturally come as your child develops. If you are at all concerned with their progress, please see your child's doctor or a professional speech therapist for further instruction.

- Speaking clearly
- Pronouncing words correctly
- Speaking in full sentences
- Developing vocabulary
- Identifying Objects/people by their names
- Expressing their own ideas
- Re-telling stories in sequence

Math readiness

For the preschooler, math includes shapes, colors, and counting. Math can be made fun by the use of things that interest your preschooler. For example, counting cars, dinosaurs, flowers, bears, and anything else that they love makes learning math so much more exciting! Keep this area fun for your preschooler and let them help you pick the manipulatives they prefer. Here is a list of some things you can work on for this age level.

- Identifying basic shapes
- Identifying basic colors

- Identifying numbers (Typically 0-10 sometimes higher for students who are ready.)
- Putting numerals in order 0-10
- Counting 0-20
- Sorting objects by size
- Understand how to graph (For example chart the weather, or sort candy by color using a graph grid, discuss which has the most, least, middle amount.)
- Say the days of the week
- Say the months of the year
- Learn terms like less, more, fewer, most
- Learn terms like above, under, over, beneath

Music & Art

I love teaching music and art to preschoolers. They're always so excited to share their creativity with others and really don't have many reservations about getting "into" their work. Preschoolers love to dance freely, and make lots of messes with all of those fun art supplies! Here is a small list of things you can work on in this area.

- Showing enthusiasm for music

- Listening to different styles of music
- Singing along
- Practicing rhythm through movement and dancing
- Using/creating instruments
- Exploring different art media
- Creating imaginative art work
- Drawing lines and shapes
- Identifying colors by name
- Interpreting pictures
- Playing with Play-Doh
- Painting
- Water Colors

Personal development

Personal development is just learning about one's own self. It is at this stage that students typically work on learning names and addresses. Here is a list of some things you can start to teach your preschooler.

- Full Name
- Address

- Telephone Number
- Birthday

Health & Wellness

Teaching children to take care of their bodies, eat well, and be physically active at a young age is a great way to help ensure they will continue with these practices once they're older.

Here are some great ideas to teach during your preschool year in regards to health.

- Learning how to bathe on their own
- Brushing their hair
- Brushing their teeth
- Washing hands
- Learn bathroom procedures
- Put on shoes
- Put on coat
- Dress for the weather
- Learn healthy vs. non-healthy food choices

Large-motor skills

Working on the larger motor skills is a great way to increase physical activity in your preschooler. It's also a wonderful way to get their wiggles out. I'll often alternate a more sedentary activity with something more active to help my preschooler focus better during our day.

Here are some things to work on:

- Walking
- Running
- Jumping
- Climbing
- Catching balls
- Throwing balls
- Increase stamina
- Showing partiality between left and right hands

Science & Nature

Preschoolers love to learn about the world around them. Adding in some age appropriate science experiments and nature walks can be a great way to help your preschooler learn to appreciate God's world. While this isn't a requirement for younger students, it can be a fun addition. Some ideas:

- Nature Walks
- Color something you see outside
- Bird Watching
- I Spy trips to the zoo, museums, parks, etc.
- Crafts using plant material
- Growing seeds
- Learn about animals and their habitats
- Learn the names of favorite plants and animals

Feel free to use the above guide to help you get started in planning a well-rounded preschool year. Remember like I said before, preschool is a year for fun and experimentation. As a homeschooler you can really tailor your preschool year towards the interests of your child and make the process of learning fun for your students.

Preschool assessment

I also have a preschool assessment form that I use to just assess where my preschooler is skill-wise during the year. We do an evaluation at the beginning of the year, then again towards the end of the year to see where we have made progress and what we need more work on. Please do not share the results with your student; there is no need to pressure them in anyway at this point. Use it as a guide for yourself so you know where your student needs more work.

There is a free preschool assessment form in the Homeschooling 101 Forms and Lesson Planner download that comes with purchase of this book.

Check out the "resources" section for a list of some of my favorite preschool products.

Chapter 13

Homeschooling Kindergarten & Elementary Students

Elementary years can be an exciting time. Students at this age are eager to learn new things, but might also start to become reluctant when things start to get harder. With homeschooling you have the flexibility to take subjects that might otherwise be somewhat boring, and turn them into hands-on type activities that make the learning process much more exciting and memorable.

Now that your student has entered into elementary school, you will need to check with your state laws regarding curriculum, subject requirements, testing, and any other regulations that might be relevant to your area. But that doesn't mean you can't take the opportunity to make it fun.

With a little bit of planning, you can add in relevant hands on projects, lap booking, note booking, field trips, science experiments, and anything else you can come up with to make learning more exciting.

The subject requirements for your elementary student will most likely depend on grade level as well as state requirements, so you'll want to check with your state laws when choosing curriculum for your elementary aged student. To help you get started, see a guide to what to teach in chapter 2 of this book on choosing curriculum.

Check out the "resources" section for more ideas to include in your studies to enhance the learning process for younger students:

Kindergarten assessment

I also have a kindergarten assessment form that I use to see how my student is progressing during the year. We do an evaluation at the beginning of the year, then again towards the end to see where we have made progress and what we need more work on.

As I mentioned in the preschool section of this book, **please do not share the results with your student**, there is no need to pressure them in anyway at this point. Use it as a guide for yourself so you know where your student needs more work.

There is a kindergarten assessment form with the free Homeschooling 101 Forms and Lesson Planner that comes with purchase of this book.

Sight word assessment

I also like to perform a sight word evaluation based on the Dolch sight word list. You can create your own if you're using another curriculum or guide for reading.

I evaluate my students based on their recognition of the word when reading it as well as their ability to spell the word correctly. I mark a word mastered if the student can read the word properly within 5 seconds.

There is a sight word assessment form that comes with the free Homeschooling 101 Forms and Lesson Planner that comes with purchase of this book.

Chapter 14

Homeschooling Jr. & High School

Homeschooling through the upper grades can be an overwhelming and intimidating thought that can create alarm in some of the most relaxed homeschooling parents. So I wanted to start off this chapter by reassuring you. Yes, YOU CAN DO IT!

Aside from the academics required, your primary goal is to prepare your student for their adult life. Homeschooling can help continue to build a bond with your student, and cement your relationship during a tumultuous time in their lives. Having a parent they can count on for training and sound advice will have eternal rewards when it comes to their future.

Homeschooling through high school…

YOU CAN DO IT!

Homeschooling through high school can also allow students to experience more things without the confinements of a classroom setting. You're free to get out and actually participate in various things that interest them, along with learning in a more hands-on fashion. You can also tailor the curriculum towards their career aspirations, and challenge them academically with accelerated programs and college level work if and when students are ready.

Socially speaking teens are also susceptive to peer-pressure, the need to fit in and conform to various "groups". At home you can create a safe learning environment where these pressures are removed. Instead your student will have the opportunity to become more self-confident in who they are and who God has created them to be.

There are several options when it comes to the demands of high school level subjects. Co-ops, online, and DVD courses are a popular choice for homeschooling through subjects that require more expertise on the part of the teacher. And don't forget to make it fun. Students at this level can help tailor a unit study or more in depth project based on their goals and interests.

There is also college dual-enrollment classes available to homeschoolers which can help students become accustomed to a classroom environment. They also give students college credit while technically still in high school.

A little planning will go a long way to creating an effective and positive high school experience for both you and your student. You will want to discuss with your student their future goals and career prospects. If college is in their future, make sure to take time to look at the entrance requirements for your prospective college so your student will be able to meet those requirements upon graduation from high school. Build your curriculum to fit your state requirements along with consideration for their future goals.

I also suggest having your students take an aptitude test during 8th grade, or prior to the start of 9th grade. This is great in helping students find strengths and interests as they prepare for their adult careers. You can find free aptitude tests online. Use the tests as a guide in helping your student, but don't let them deter students from pursing their interests.

Here are some things to keep in mind when preparing to homeschool your high school student:

- Transcripts and Record Keeping
- College Entrance Requirements

- Career Goals
- Student Interests (Consider having your student help tailor their year towards their goals.)

More Helpful Information:

- HSLDA Homeschooling High school
- FastWeb.com - A great resource for homeschooling through high school and preparing college bound students.
- The Home Scholar
- Donna Young High School Forms
- Homeschooling the Teen Years by Cafi Cohen

Chapter 15

Homeschooling on a Budget

Homeschooling is flexible in so many ways, and that includes budgetary concerns. There are many options for homeschooling on a budget. Here are some things to consider when creating a homeschooling budget:

- Curriculum (most likely the greatest expense)
- Testing Fees
- Printing or Copying Costs
- Building a Home Library
- School Supplies
- Extracurricular activities or lessons
- Annual State Conventions
- Technology Aids

Use your library

Not only does the library have an expansive selection of materials, it can be successfully used to build an entire curriculum if you take the time. Along with books, libraries also include videos, audio resources, discussion groups, lectures, and topical classes as well. With inter-library loans you can really get ahold of almost any resources you may need.

The library can be a valuable tool in not only keeping your book costs down, but also in aiding your unit studies.

Field trips: A hands on learning tool

Chances are there are several educational opportunities within the rich resources of your local community. A little research can go a long way to creating memorable hands on educational trips for your students. As you create your schedule for the year, make a list of field trips that will enhance your learning. Before showing up, contact the coordinator for the site. Many places offer a discount for homeschooling families or groups.

Don't forget to check with local companies, many offer free tours of their facilities. For example our local nursery offers free tours along with a project for small groups. We were able to get a tour of the grounds along with a personal guide who explained all about various plants, soil types, and plant care. We finished our tour with a hands-on activity where the students each potted their own small plant to take home.

Homeschooling groups and co-ops

Homeschooling co-ops are a great way to meet other homeschoolers, as well as pool resources. Many offer activities like spelling bees, presentation days, and geography and science fairs. Some even offer a variety of classes where students are able to use a more expensive curriculum at a discounted rate. And still others offer things like computer classes and science labs that would otherwise be too expensive for one family to afford. By making use of a co-op you can also draw on the expertise of other homeschooling parents, create opportunities for new friendships among students, and parents alike. See chapter 18 for some group and co-op ideas.

Buy used

Regardless of our income, we all want to get a good deal on school materials. Whenever possible we purchase used teacher's manuals, student text books, and supplies. Not only does buying used save money, but it also makes parting with materials that aren't working for your family less painful!

Here are some places where you can find great prices on new and used materials:

- Homeschool Classifieds – An online forum where homeschoolers can buy and sell curriculum
- eBay
- Local Used Curriculum Fairs (Do an internet search for used fairs in your area.)
- Half Price Books
- Half.Com
- Amazon – Amazon is a great place to find used materials
- Christian Book – Low prices on educational resources
- Rainbow Resource – Low prices on educational resources

Use free resources

Along with the local library, the internet can be a very valuable tool for homeschooling on a budget. Not only can you research just about anything you want to for free, there are also several blogs and websites that offer free printables for a variety of topics. Here are some of my favorites:

- Confessions of a Homeschooler – Homeschooling ideas, curriculum, and tips!
- Deep Space Sparkle – Free online art lessons and activities for all ages.
- Donna Young – A variety of free homeschooling forms, planners, calendars, and lesson ideas.
- Homeschool Share – Free online resource for lapbooking and unit studies.
- KB Teachers – Free online worksheets
- Lapbook Lessons – Free online lapbooking resources
- Ambleside Online – Full online curriculum using the Charlotte Mason method of learning
- Homeschool Freebie of the Day – Subscribers receive a new homeschool freebie each day
- Starfall – Excellent site for teaching reading skills to younger learners

- Spelling City – A free online spelling & vocabulary website. You can use their lists, or create your own

Borrow & Trade

One of the least expensive ways to acquire homeschooling materials is to trade with other homeschoolers. Ask your friends to see if they're willing to loan out some of their unused curriculum for the year and offer to trade with them in return. If you do borrow items from others, be diligent to keep them in good condition and return the materials immediately upon completion, or an agreed upon time.

If you loan out your materials, make sure to make a list of items borrowed, and write your name inside all of your items as well. It's easy for materials to get mixed in with everything else once school starts, so making sure you have labeled your items well is helpful.

Have a good plan

If you've laid out your curriculum plan as directed in previous chapters, you will be much less likely to waste your money on spur of the moment purchases. Once you decide on your curriculum stick to that plan and don't veer off unless you really decide it's worth it.

Re-use & Recycle

This goes for clothes, curriculum, storage containers, and anything else we can re-purpose. We pass down most of the curriculum from our oldest to the younger students as they get there. That way each year we are only purchasing materials for our oldest student and consumables for the younger ones.

Consider recycling your consumables if appropriate. Having children write answers in a composition book can allow the reuse of a workbook for future students.

Instead of buying fancy storage containers, shelving units, and school supplies, look for used or free. Garage Sales, Good Will, Craig's List, and eBay are all wonderful ways to find furniture, and other school goodies at a great price.

Selling curriculum

Selling old curriculum, school supplies, etc. is a wonderful way to re-coop some of the money you have spent along the way. It's also a great way to help other homeschoolers who are just starting out. The practice of swapping curriculum is a common one and can benefit both sides. Here are some ideas to help you unload your used materials:

- Have a garage sale
- Host a table at a used curriculum fair
- List items on Homeschool Classifieds, Amazon Marketplace, or eBay

.

Chapter 16

Starting Homeschool Midyear

One of the most frequently asked questions I receive is how to go about starting mid-year. It's more common than you think to pull students out mid-year and begin the homeschooling journey.

As a homeschooler you have the flexibility to start at any time of the year. Most families choose to start homeschooling at semester break, but you can make the change anytime you feel it is necessary for your family.

Know your state law

If you are considering removing your student from public or private school during the school year, you'll want to check with your state laws regarding this process. In most states you will be required to send in a withdrawal form to your school district, and then submit either a Notice of Intent to homeschool, or enrollment in an umbrella or independent school that allows work to be done at home.

You may also be required to submit a list of your continuing curriculum choices, a copy of your diploma, and any other paperwork that may be required prior to withdrawing your student from school.

Don't forget about testing and evaluations if they are required for this school year as well.

Discuss the withdrawal

Along with discussing the timing of the withdrawal with your spouse (if possible), you'll also want to discuss it with your student so that the decision isn't unexpected. Help pick a date that works best for your family and proceed from there.

Get records from the school

Make sure to get whatever records you need from your school. That may include transcripts, attendance records, as well as immunization reports and anything else they may have on file for your student.

Set up a daily schedule

You'll want to create a basic schedule for your new homeschool day. Having a basic plan in writing will aid in the transition process. It will also help you stay on track and feel like you are getting necessary things accomplished. Even if you don't stick to your schedule like glue, having something basic in writing will greatly aid in the organization of your school. You'll also want to discuss your new homeschooling plan with your student so they know what will be expected of them when they make the transition from school to home.

Get involved

Take a little time to research the local homeschooling groups and co-ops in your area. While it is not a requirement to participate in a homeschooling group, it can be very helpful when first starting out. Getting to know other homeschoolers helps you feel like you are not alone in this journey. They can also help you with questions, concerns, and general support and encouragement.

Allow time to adjust

You can expect a period of adjustment whenever bringing a child out of a school setting into your home. You might need to begin slowly to give your student time to get used to the new schedule. If your student was behind previously, you might also need to spend some time getting caught up on basic skills that slipped through the cracks in the school system. Don't be afraid to go back a grade level, or at least to a skill that they missed and start over so you can be sure they understand before moving forward.

There may also be a season of "deprogramming" that you will have to go through with your student. You may need to break old habits they may have fallen into, or even encourage them that they can be successful in something they were previously struggling with.

Keep it simple

Since you are starting mid-year, you probably have not had adequate time to plan an entire curriculum. I suggest keeping things manageable at first until everyone gets used to the change. Make sure to focus on core subjects. If your student had something that was working well for them in the school, consider using that curriculum for the rest of the year to make the transition a little smoother for them.

You can refer to the previous chapters in this book to help you get started. You'll also want to set up a school area in your home. You don't have to have an entire room, but you will want a designated space for your student to work.

Sign up for extracurricular activities

If your student was participating in extracurricular activities sponsored by the school, you may want to take some time to research how to continue with these. Some school districts will allow homeschool students to continue to participate in a sport. Depending on the reason you are withdrawing from school, you may not want to continue with the school district you were previously associated with. In that case there are usually several other options for homeschoolers including local competitive and recreational leagues for most sports and extracurricular activities.

Chapter 17

Switching Curriculum Midyear

Sometimes it happens that we find ourselves needing to switch something mid-year. For me it was about three months into our 3rd year of homeschooling when I realized that our math curriculum was not working.

So what do you do? Especially when you've spent more than you wanted on something only to find it isn't a good fit? Well, you switch to something else. Freedom is one of the many gifts that come with homeschooling. We are free to choose curriculum that best fits the needs of our family.

Sometimes things can seem like a great choice. But then when put into action they just don't work like you had hoped. And despite all of our careful research in choosing curriculum, we can choose things that don't work for us. Don't feel bad about switching mid-year. We have all had things we've needed to change during our year to better our homeschooling experience.

Taking into consideration cost, you might want to take some time to see if you can modify the current curriculum to work for the rest of the year. If it is not working and causing you too much unneeded stress, then I suggest you look into switching to something else.

While you don't want to make your children think that you are willing to switch out curriculum anytime they don't love something, sometimes switching is a must. Other times we need to persevere and be diligent with what we've chosen if there is good cause.

"Don't feel bad about switching mid-year. We have all had things we've needed to change during our year to better our homeschooling experience."

In our 3rd year math disaster, it became apparent that we needed to switch to something else. At first I was reluctant to make a change so far into another curriculum. I like to finish curriculum. Quitting something half-way through, and not having time to finish the new one, didn't exactly leave me with a warm fuzzy feeling.

But for my children's sake, and the sake of my own sanity, I sat down and ordered something else. The day it arrived was one of the happiest days in my homeschooling career. I removed the old books, and opened our new books. That small act saved the future of our homeschooling journey. There was an immediate release of stress for me, and my children were also happy with the change. Things have been great ever since, and we aren't looking back.

What about the old curriculum? You can always recover some of your costs by selling the old curriculum at a used fair, or online. Or maybe it just isn't a good fit right now, and can be saved for a later time.

Whatever your reasons are for switching curriculum mid-year, know that it is okay. Make your decisions based on the needs of your family. Curriculum varies in style and method, so trying new things is a great way to enhance your learning experience and make your homeschool successful. Finding a curriculum that fits your needs can make the difference between hating and loving learning.

Chapter 18

Homeschooling an Only Child

Typically when we think of homeschooling, we envision a larger family. But that's just a stereotype; there are many families who choose to homeschool an only child. Don't be intimidated by the size of your family, large or small, you can homeschool if you are committed! Not only do you have the added benefit of truly being able to tailor your curriculum to your child, but your child will also benefit from one-on-one teaching.

I know socialization can rear its ugly head in this situation, as well. But keep in mind the secret to socialization is teaching your child to get along with people of all ages. And depending on where you live, your child probably already has a group of friends and activities that they are participating in.

Here are a few ideas to help enhance homeschooling an only child.

Include the whole family

Sometimes doing a science project is just more fun with other people. Include both parents in a fun science experiment. Take nature walks as a family and have everyone keep a journal of what they find on the walks. Go on field trips together, do art projects, and read books together. You might also consider encouraging your student to give a presentation to both parents in the evening or invite grandparents or friends over to listen. Have your student stand in front of the room, state their name and age, then give their presentation. Allow them to answer questions and take comments after their presentation is complete.

Join a co-op

Joining a co-op is beneficial for both the only child as well as the parent. Co-ops can often provide lessons that a parent might not be able to do on their own. And they create an environment where parents and students can get to know other homeschoolers and form relationships. Visit www.HSLDA.org or do an online search for homeschool co-ops in your area.

Provide opportunities for independent studies

While homeschooling creates a beautiful bond between a parent and a child, taking a break from the intensity of the one-on-one teaching time is also a valuable tool. Choose some curriculum that allows your student to work more independently wherever it makes the most sense. Doing so will give you and your child a small break from each other during the day.

Offer to host a small group activity

There are a number of small group ideas that can augment your homeschool. Offering to host for a group of similarly aged children is a great way to create lasting friendships and a fun learning environment as well. It is great for activities that are better suited to groups as opposed to individual study.

You will probably be able to enlist the help of the other parents who will be attending as well. Have them alternate bringing a snack to the group meeting, providing materials, or even teaching a lesson. Most families are happy to get involved if someone else takes the lead! Here are a few small group ideas to help you get started.

LEGO Club

Each month host a group for Lego Club. Send out a theme for the month via email to the participants. Have students bring a small baggie of spare Lego's for a challenge round. Have students give a presentation on their creation. Allow for other students to comment or ask questions following the presentation. After all students have presented their creation, give them a quick idea for a 5 minute challenge round. For example have them create an object to help get a cat out of a tree, but it can't be a ladder. Give them 5 minutes to create something from their spare Lego's then give a short presentation on their creation. Offer a small snack then free play time afterwards to help students bond, and provide an opportunity for parents to mingle, as well.

Keepers of the Home

This is a Christian group for mothers and daughters. Group leaders pick activities for the group of girls then teach a lesson at a host home. Typically mothers take turns hosting and leading each meeting. You can organize the group however best fits your needs. You can find more information on this group at Confessions of a Homeschooler.

Contenders of the Faith

Contenders is a Christian group for fathers and sons. It is similar to the Keepers group in that the fathers take turns hosting and teaching various activities. It is a wonderful experience for the children, and also creates a unique bond between fathers and sons as the fathers train their sons in righteousness.

Science Club

Offer to host a monthly science club where students gather for fun and educational science experiments. You can gather various experiment ideas using any number of resources such as your local library, or internet related searches.

Book Club

Depending on the ages of your students you can offer to host a book club. You might consider having the students all read a certain amount of chapters then come together to discuss it. There might even be a related activity you can do to go along with the book as well. For younger students, consider offering a read-a-loud time where they gather to listen to a story together. You can have them dress up to match the theme or offer a small craft to go with your story afterwards. As with the other groups, offer a free play time afterwards for both children and parents to fellowship.

Classic Literature Club

Reading through classic literature together is a great way to not only encourage the classics, but also share insight with fellow peers. Offer to host a classic literature group and have students read assigned chapters in your book, then gather together for a discussion and activity. Great resources for these are my Classic Literature Unit Studies.

Art Group

Offer to host a group that focuses on a different artist or art project each month. You can ask the other members to help provide supplies, and materials to help you with cost. A resource for group art lessons can be found in the book "How to Teach Art to Children", and the website Deep Space Sparkle. If you prefer to do an artist study, the World's Greatest Artists Vol. 1 and World's Greatest Artists Vol. 2 is a great option for group lessons!

PE Group

One of the hardest subjects to include in a typical homeschooling environment can be physical education. While we can encourage our children to participate in extracurricular activities, hosting a P.E. group with friends is a great way to add some exercise and fun to your homeschool! One of my favorite physical education programs is the Family Time

Fitness program. The lessons come with step by step instructions as well as video examples to help you. It would be a great activity to do as a group.

Geography Group

Gather once a month with a group of friends and focus on a new country each time. Have students dress to match the culture, as well as bring fun recipes that are authentic to the region you are learning about. Gather a few books to read to the group, and any other fun materials. Then end the meeting with a party to honor the country you have studied. A great resource for your trip around the world is the Expedition Earth world geography curriculum.

Provide extracurricular activities

Ask your child what they are interested in and then see what extracurricular type activities are available in your area. Groups like Awanas or various local recreational sports are a great resource for getting your child involved in activities. Most areas offer a variety of sports and leisure activities to encourage students in their goals. If you have older students you might want to look into your local school district or city recreation center to see what sports opportunities are available for homeschooled students.

Change your location

Every so often taking your schoolwork to a new location can be a great way to break up the monotony of learning at home. Changing location is also a great way to teach students how to work with distractions. In an only child environment it is easy to control the noise level so students get used to working in a nice quiet atmosphere. And while this is a benefit to your child, learning to focus through distractions can also be a valuable skill.

Take field trips

A quick phone call to a friend can make a field trip a lot more fun! And if you can plan the trip to coordinate with your current line of study, it will be educational too!

As you can see, homeschooling an only child doesn't need to be boring or lonely. Instead you have the unique blessing of being able to focus on your child's needs more directly. You can choose your pace and tailor your curriculum to the unique needs of your student. And there are a variety of options for you to provide a quality education for your child, as well as get them involved in outside activities, that will encourage positive friendships to last a lifetime!

Chapter 19

Homeschooling & the Working Parent

Homeschooling itself is a full time job, so carefully consider whether or not working and homeschooling is a realistic choice for your family.

While homeschooling doesn't take the same amount of time as classroom teaching does, you will still need to follow your state requirements for attendance and annual hours. And regardless of your student's ages, it will also require a certain amount of daily commitment on your part.

That said, "Yes! You can homeschool and work". But make no mistake…it isn't going to be easy.

There are a couple reasons why someone may need to homeschool and work. The most common occurrence is the single parent. Others may be concerned that they won't be able to make it on one salary. Whatever your reason, there are several families who have found ways to both homeschool and work.

If you are in the camp of having two working parents, I encourage you to consider your budget priorities and see if there is a way to get by on one salary. As I said before homeschooling is a full time career choice, and you may find that you can get by on one salary by making some adjustments to your family's budget, or even pairing down to part-time work as opposed to full-time.

Here are a few helpful tips to make homeschooling and working easier.

Pray

Most importantly pray for God to reveal His will for your family. If He is calling you to homeschool, He will also provide you with the means to do that. It will most likely mean making some changes, but with Christ all things are possible. He will make a way for your homeschooling journey if you allow Him to.

Look for a job that is flexible

As most of you know, I am author of the homeschooling blog www.confessionsofahomeschooler.com. While I didn't originally intend this to become a career path, thanks to my readers, it has on some level become a "job". Thankfully being "self-employed" as such, I can set my own hours. That means I am free to homeschool during the day, and then work in the evenings.

If you already have a job, talk to your boss and see if there is a way you can work from home part time, or if they will allow you to adjust your hours so it better fits your homeschooling needs. If possible, arrange your schedule and your spouse's schedule, so parents can co-teach. That way they will both be involved in the homeschooling process.

If you are passionate about homeschooling, but find it isn't feasible in your current job, consider finding a new job that will better fit your goals.

Create a realistic schedule

Keep in mind your unique situation and help create a schedule that fits both the needs of your work and your homeschool. The time of day which you do school is typically not mandated by most state regulations, so getting out of the traditional school schedule may go a long way in helping you successfully homeschool. If your career requires you work during the day, consider doing school in the afternoons, evenings, or on weekends. When you're a homeschooling and working parent, flexibility is your best friend!

Use curriculum that matches your needs

If you need to work full time consider using an online homeschooling curriculum, or DVD curriculum. While this certainly works better for older students, it can greatly help the working and homeschooling parent. Another option is to choose curriculum that does not require a large amount of pre-planning on your part to make your schooling easier.

Plan ahead

It is essential for the working parent to plan ahead. Having your homeschooling day well planned and setup for your student will go a long way to getting school completed each day. This will require preparation on your part, but the more work you do ahead of time, the less chaos will ensue during school time.

Consider getting help

If your job requires you work during the day, you might want to consider hiring a helper to look after your children while you work. If you cannot work from home, you will need to arrange somewhere for your children to go during the day while you are away.

You'll also want to consider basic house duties. Can you split them up between the members of your family, or will you need to get help with housework, laundry, and meals? One good way to help with meal time is to consider once-a-month cooking, and freezer meals. Having dinners prepared ahead of time is a great way to alleviate some of the stress of a working parent!

If possible enlist a friend or family member to help take your children to extracurricular activities.

Homeschool co-ops

Homeschool co-ops are a great way to give you some time off while also giving your children the opportunity to partake in classes you might not be able to do at home. Some co-ops require parent participation, while others allow you to drop off students. Most offer social activities for students such as field trips, spelling bees, geography and science fairs, as well as homeschooling parent nights where you can develop friendships and support for your homeschooling journey.

Chapter 20

Homeschooling & Special Needs

First off I want to encourage you that you are not alone! There are several families that have chosen to homeschool children with special needs. The needs may range from something such as attention deficit disorder to children with more severe and multiple handicaps.

Often bringing special needs children home to be educated is a wonderful way to reach an otherwise reluctant student. As their parent you can offer your student the security, stability, flexibility, and encouragement they need to be successful.

While I do not personally have special needs students there are a wide variety of websites and information available to homeschooling your students.

Here is a list of top websites to help those of you needing direction in this area.

- Autism Speaks: www.autismspeaks.org
- Dianne Craft: www.diannecraft.org – Working with struggling learners
- Family Education:www.school.familyeducation.com – Homeschooling your special needs child
- Handwriting Without Tears: www.hwtears.com/ - Program developed by an occupational therapist and handwriting specialist
- HSLDA: www.hslda.org
- Laureate Special Needs Software: www.laureatelearning.com - Offers a variety of programs for language acquisition.
- List of National Organizations: www.hslda.org
- NATHHAN: www.nathhan.com – National Challenged Homeschools Associated network
- NHEN: www.nhen.org - Library of Special Needs Articles
- NorCal Center on Deafness, Inc: www.norcalcenter.org - Offers workshops, social events, and a summer camp for the deaf and hard of hearing

- PACE: www.tckconsultant.org – Special Needs Education
- Sensory Processing Disorder Foundation: www.spdfoundation.net
- Special Needs Homeschooling: networkedblogs.com

Chapter 21

What about Socialization?

One of the first questions I am asked regarding homeschooling is…"What about socialization?"

I almost hesitate to even include this chapter in my book. But I know for new homeschoolers, the issue of socialization can be one of their main concerns.

Just so we're all on the same page, let's define socialization. According to the dictionary, socialization is defined as a process whereby an individual acquires the knowledge, language, social skills, values, and behavior to conform to the norms of a group or community.

For homeschoolers, that translates into whether or not our children will be able to succeed in their adult life.

Studies have repeatedly shown that homeschoolers on average outperform their public school peers, not only academically, but socially too. Homeschoolers tend to have more self-confidence as well. They are also shown to score approximately 37 points higher on standardized achievement tests than the public school student average. *(Statistics taken from www.hslda.org.)*

Academically homeschooled students have continued to show excellence through their scores. But what about their ability to succeed as adults? Many fear that by choosing to homeschool their children, they will by default isolate them from the outside world. And in turn, raise children who are not prepared for adulthood.

Due to sheer circumstances, the public school environment tends to lend itself to encouraging students to conform to their peers. Conversely, homeschooling parents focus more on teaching their students responsibility, character, service, compassion, and other essential life skills that will benefit them in their adult life.

Since homeschooling parents are more able to focus on social and emotional characteristics of their children, youth are more likely to model the behavior of their parent. Public schooled students more often emulate the values and conduct of their peers. With more parental involvement in their upbringing, studies have indicated that homeschooled students show less behavioral issues than those in the public school system.

Another advantage we have as homeschoolers is the freedom to tailor our curriculum. We have the opportunity to expose our students to education through field trips, hands-on learning tools, and pursue things that interest them more freely than their publically schooled peers.

We also have the opportunity to participate in a wide variety of community groups, clubs, and sports activities. Things like church youth groups, Awanas, local clubs, art classes, book clubs, science clubs, homeschool co-ops, physical education classes, local community groups, and dozens more, are all excellent ways for homeschoolers to avoid the issue of being socially isolated. *For more group activity ideas see chapter 18.*

As homeschoolers we are not required to chain our students to desks all day. Instead we can experience the world around us more freely. This flexibility provides the homeschooled student with a well-rounded and balanced educational experience.

Your commitment

Now, I realize that I can spout off statistics to you all day. But the socialization of your student will ultimately come down to your commitment as a homeschooling parent. While all of these wonderful opportunities are available to most homeschoolers, as a parent you will be responsible for getting your students involved in the various activities and experiences that are available to you.

I have to be honest; at the beginning of our homeschooling journey I too was concerned about the issue of socialization. Since then, I've learned that socialization is a myth at best. It's usually an issue that is brought up by those who aren't fully educated regarding homeschooling, and those who don't support the concept.

> "My husband and I affectionately refer to this time as "the year we over-socialized".

Due to my fear of raising un-socialized children, during our first year of homeschooling I enrolled our children in a variety of groups, and extracurricular activities. My husband and I affectionately refer to this time as "the year we over-socialized".

Since then I've learned that it is okay not to participate in every single thing out there. We've paired down our involvement to include only the things that make sense for our family, and activities that are of true interest to our family.

Over the years, I've come to realize that our children are doing just fine. They get along well with others, are good at working as a team, and are able to successfully interact well with people of all ages. They are also more self-confident and don't usually worry as much about what other people think. Instead, they focus on their own goals and ambitions. And every so often, they even honor the needs of others above their own.

After 7 years of homeschooling, I still struggle with self-doubt, and I still worry about my children's future. As a parent, I don't think it would be any different regardless of our educational choices.

But God has been good to show me bits and pieces of how we are eternally affecting our children through our decision to homeschool. I've had people comment on how well my children play together, how polite they are, or how nice it was when they held the door for someone.

I've seen them be the "peace-maker" in a difficult situation, and watched as my older children have helped a younger one. I've observed as they play with friends including their younger siblings without issue.

While our daily life isn't always blissfully free of behavioral issues, I can see glimpses of the people that they're growing into. I have witnessed positive character traits emerging, and I can rest knowing that they'll be well prepared for adulthood, and eternity.

Ways to get involved

If you would like some information on extracurricular options for homeschoolers, here are a few ideas to help get you started.

- Keepers at Home: www.keepersofthefaith.com
- Contenders of the Faith: www.keepersofthefaith.com
- Science Clubs
- Book Clubs
- Literature Clubs
- National Competition groups
- Team Sports
- High School Sports (Most local high schools offer spots to homeschooled students who qualify.)
- PE Classes
- Homeschool Co-ops (Search your local area and "homeschool group" for a listing.)

- Civic Organizations (Fire Stations, Libraries, hospitals, businesses, etc. usually offer tours for homeschool groups.)
- Local Museums
- YMCA: www.ymca.net
- Dance, music, art, ceramics, and drama classes via your local community education center.
- Field Trips
- Reading programs
- Community theatre
- Community volunteers programs
- Chess clubs
- Computer club
- Speech and Debate clubs

For more detailed information regarding homeschooling and socialization visit the HSLDA Socialization webpage.

Chapter 22

Time Management & Keeping your Sanity

Good time management for homeschoolers is a necessity. You've already seen a sample of our daily schedule. But there are a few more tips I'd like to share with you on the topic of time management and keeping your sanity.

First of all, no one can "do it all" so to speak. Something usually has to give when you're juggling homeschooling, running a household, parenting children, being a spouse, serving in ministry, and working.

Remember, the only pressure we're under is pressure we've put on ourselves.

If your schedule is too hectic, take a minute *(I know, I know, you don't have a minute, but trust me this will help.)* and write down all your commitments. Next see what you can get rid of, and what is necessary, and then make any necessary changes to your schedule.

Having some sort of routine that you follow will go a long way to helping you stay above water. And good time management is crucial to both your mental and physical well-being.

Here are some tips to help keep things organized and running smoothly.

Set a basic family schedule

Setting a basic routine that your family follows can be a vital element to your homeschooling journey. For example dictating Monday as laundry day, Tuesday as bathrooms, and so on can help you stay on top of things instead of feeling like you're drowning in a sea of tasks. You can rest, knowing at some point during the week, everything will get taken care of.

Delegate household tasks

If everyone is chipping in to help, chores won't seem so daunting. Don't be fooled by the younger ages of your children. Teaching them life skills even at an early age is entirely appropriate and also gives them a sense of worth and belonging in your family unit. For example children as young as four years old can help fold laundry, put away dishes, set the table. You'll want to help supervise most of these, but then you'll notice by the time they are 5 or so they'll start being able to do these things more independently.

Keep things simple

Set expectations based on the needs of your family. Pairing down on activities, or labor intensive curriculum, might just save some of your sanity on a day to day basis.

Plan ahead

I've already talked about planning ahead for your school year, but I really can't stress it enough. Being organized is extremely helpful in getting through a homeschooling year. When we don't plan ahead we find ourselves flying by the seat of our pants, unprepared for activities, and sometimes even in a state of chaos in the classroom as we're scrounging for supplies and materials. Meanwhile students slowly lose focus waiting for us.

If you've planned ahead and done your job well, then the homeschooling part is a matter of following a preset plan. You will find yourself much more prepared, and much less stressed.

And no, I don't follow my schedule to an exact tee, but knowing that I've set forth a well-planned year, I'm much less likely to become discouraged or feel like I'm failing my children in our homeschooling journey.

Set your priorities

Decide what will be priorities for your family and focus on those first. Once you have taken care of the big things, you can have the freedom to welcome other smaller things into your day knowing that you've met your major goals. If you decide to let something minor go that day, it will be okay as you've taken care of the things you previously set forth as a priority.

With homeschooling it is common to feel like you've got a thousand plates spinning all at once and can't seem to keep up. For a homeschooler this can be an overwhelming thought, with the big question being "how do I keep all my plates from falling?"

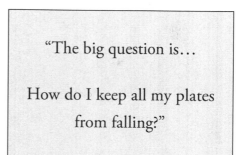

"The big question is…

How do I keep all my plates from falling?"

In other words, how do we keep our heads above water in a world that seems to be crashing in around us? (*I just want to be clear that this isn't some fool-proof master plan, it's just how I keep those little men in little white coats from coming to take me away.*)

First, list your plates

Take a few minutes and list all of the things you have going on right now that require your attention. Here are mine…God, husband, Strawberry Shortcake, Turbo, Tinker Bell, the Teeny Tot, homeschool & school planning, family time, animals (2 dogs, 1 cat, 4 fish, 1 hamster), cooking, cleaning, laundry, extracurricular activities, blogging, time with friends, and me time *(yeah right…).*

Second, prioritize

Take a few minutes to list your priorities as well as your commitments mentioned previously. Take care of the big priorities first, and then let the rest fit in where they can. You can see how I have set up the priorities for our family below.

And finally… simplify

Take a look at all of your plates, pray for wisdom to know what God has for you right now, and what He doesn't. Don't waste your time on things that God isn't in, you'll just be spinning your plates in vain! *Psalm 127:1 "Unless the LORD builds the house, its builders labor in vain."*

Here is a list of our priorities to help you get started. Of course this is just a guide. Your reasons for homeschooling may differ greatly as every home has unique needs.

1. God: "But seek first His kingdom and His righteousness, and all these things will be given to you as well." *Matthew 6:33*

At times like this it's important to keep things in perspective. If everything else gets pushed aside today, will it really matter? So what if the laundry sits for the day? So what if I order in food instead of making dinner here and there? So what if we take a day off school?

Really, in order to keep all the plates of life spinning, we have to make priorities. The first one **must** be time with God. Setting a priority on God's will for our lives will naturally pass down to your children as they see *you* spending regular time with Him. In regards to homeschool, if we don't get anything else done, I at least try to make it a priority that we do our Bible time. Now, I'm preaching to myself here, because for me this is the easiest to let slide, and I can easily forget about it until I go to bed, then instantly I realize that I forgot to do my devotion. I've made a deal with myself that if this happens, I will get up, turn on the light and do it, right then and there. Better late than never I say. *I also use this motto to justify starting school late.* A great resource for being in the word daily is the Daily Audio Bible, and they have a Kids Daily Audio Bible too!

2. Husband: This is important parents; husbands/wives must come before kids. And I think it's important for kids to see that your husband/wife has priority. Your spouse will be there long after the kids are gone, and while there is a definite season when kids seem to prevail in order due to sheer necessity, it's still important to recognize that your spouse should be your priority.

Marriage was the first institution created by God... "For this reason a man will leave his father and mother and be united to his wife, and they will become one flesh." Genesis 2:24

Therefore, if God placed that importance on marriage, than so shall we! When my husband comes home, he tries to greet me first, then the kids. After that the kids are sent to the other room to play for a few minutes so we can have some time to discuss whatever is needed without yelling over all the loudness that comes with having four children. *(Well, except for the Teeny Tiny*

Tot, nothing can keep her from her daddy when he first walks in.
Did I mention my other motto: "blessed are the flexible"?)

3. Children: These little guys are nothing more than treasures in heaven! It is our job to "Train a child in the way he should go, and when he is old he will not turn from it." Proverbs 22:6

God has given us the greatest gift ever, and it blows my mind that He's entrusted *us* to raise one of his precious children, not to mention four of them! Sometimes I just scratch my head and wonder what God was doing when He made this choice, but then I'm reminded that He knows what He's doing regardless of whether or not I do! And Praise God for that! I try to make an effort to spend a little bit of time each day 1-on-1 with each child. It can be as easy as sitting my 4 year old on the counter to keep me company while I make dinner, to reading with my 7 year old at night. Whatever it is, take a couple minutes each day to personally tell your children that you love spending time with them!

4. Homeschool: We truly believe we are called to homeschool our children, you can read more about why we homeschool on my website under the "About Us" page. But I will say this; giving priority to homeschool has GREATLY impacted the quality and flow of our days. Previously, I was in denial, telling myself if it didn't go well, we'd just put our children in public school. Finally I came to accept our choice and really made getting school done a priority. We do it first in our day, we are flexible, but mostly we do school before anything else. That includes phone calls, emails, blogging, errand running, etc.

As mentioned previously, we made a daily schedule and try to stick to it. I don't want to be so inflexible with our day that I quench the Holy Spirit moving in our day, so that said; I try to be flexible, praying for the Lord to order our steps for the day before I get out of bed. Getting school done early, also provides for fun free time in the afternoons, and also relieves the sense of unfinished school work "looming" over us all day long.

5. **Homeschool Planning:** As stated in #4, I make homeschooling a priority every year. Along with that came some planning. I'd previously put this off just out of the sheer overwhelming feeling from organizing it all. But I set aside some time each week for planning time. This has proved to be invaluable in making our days run smoother as well as feeling like

we are actually accomplishing something. I think having a plan and not sticking to it, is far superior to having no plan to start with! *But that's just me and how I roll.*

So that's 5 plates to be running back and forth between so far... (Really 8 if you divide up the kids.) Now, I frankly feel this is enough to keep one busy enough, but I'll still address the others I listed, just because they're a part of our lives, and because, sadly, I can't really stop cooking, cleaning or doing laundry!

6. Animal Duty (2 Dogs, 1 cat, 4 fish, and 1 hamster): This one was easy...I delegate! I have 4 kids; surely they can manage to feed the animals! Presto, one less plate for mom! Go Me! It also provided a stepping block to our new chore chart. We reward the kids with a quarter for each chore they choose to complete. No one is required to work here since they're still young, but they can earn money for things if they so choose. *You can find a copy of our chore chart on my website under "Mom Tips".* They learn to earn, save, and work as a team to help out mom and dad. And the less chores mom has to do alone, the more time she has to play with the kiddos. This is a good motivator, because after all, most kids want your time.

7. Cooking: You might want to consider monthly meal planning or freezer meals to help you get through long homeschool days. I have a friend who spends one day a month cooking freezer meals, and then doesn't cook the rest of the month! I haven't been able to accomplish this just yet, but if you have a friend it'd be a fun mom's day and a great way to get some serious prepared dinners done! Here are some websites to help you get started:

- My Monthly Meal Planning: www.confessionsofahomeschooler.com/blog/tag/monthly-meal-plan
- eMeals: e-mealz.com/amember/go.php?r=252457&i=b3
- Once A Month Cooking: www.once-a-month-cookingworld.com
- Crockpot Recipes: southernfood.about.com/library/crock/blcpidx.htm

8. Family Time: In today's society, this has to be a priority! Since my husband is away from home working all day, we do our best to make sure we eat dinner each night as a family. We also have a bedtime routine which we try to follow.

I stress "try" because it doesn't always go down like this, but like I say *"Better to have a plan and not follow it, than to not have a plan at all!"* Our goal is for both my husband and I to do bedtime together. We give baths, brush teeth, cuddle with the kids, etc. Then we all gather as a family on our bed and read a family devotion, pray, then off to bed for the munchkins. I think it's all too easy to forgo family time and let everyone do their own activities without realizing the long term effects this can have on your relationships. Dinner time is also a great way to gather the whole family.

9. **Cleaning:** I happen to be a neat freak, and I can't handle clutter. This proves to be a challenge with the whole homeschooling thing; however, it also helps to keep our house somewhat orderly. We do a fun thing called **"Ten Minute Tidy"**; this is where we run around like mad putting away anything found on the floor before Daddy gets home. We set a timer and it's like a race!

Now before you start thinking I'm a supermom, let me assure you that I am not! And I'd bet my bottom dollar that, at the end of the day there's at least 1 toy on the floor in each room, even if it's hidden under the couch.

For our main household cleaning, we work as a team. The older children help with vacuuming, dusting, and general housework, cleaning their rooms, dishes, etc. I'm not a child laborer; we work as a team in our home. I do major things like toilets, mopping, and overall vacuuming. A great resource for organizing your cleaning schedule is The Fly Lady, if you have issues in this area, she's

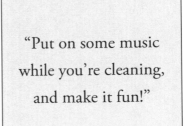

"Put on some music while you're cleaning, and make it fun!"

great! Another fun thing to do is put on some music while you're cleaning, and make it fun!

10. Laundry…oh the dreaded laundry! Even after explaining to my kids that they don't need to change 5 times a day, they still seem to rack up the piles. Now that they're a *little* older, the 5 and 6 year old have to help out putting their own clothes away. Laundry is an important life skill, so I did teach my 6 year old how to run the washer and dryer. However I usually supervise this as pouring liquid soap into the washing machine cup seems to be so much fun that one doesn't want to stop pouring even though the "fill to here" line has clearly been reached.

I'm sure people handle this differently, however I chose to do 1 load a day. It's not as overwhelming as doing 20 loads on Sat. and it's less scary for the kids (and me) to put away a couple outfits as opposed to a whole week's worth!

11. Kid's Activities: We decided to allow our children to do one activity at a time each. Since we homeschool, we are more flexible for things that meet during the daytime. My son prefers sports, so that tends to be evenings and sometimes weekends. While we allow our children to do extracurricular activities we are also careful to make sure we have family time together with Daddy. We also don't want to be consistently rushing from one thing to the next, thereby causing "stress" for our children and me. And just to recap…it's called "Homeschooling", not "Car-schooling."

12. And, finally….time with friends and ME time! Sorry, but I've searched diligently, and unfortunately *me time* is nowhere to be found in the Bible! Well, technically it is there, it's just listed as "selfishness". The good news here is that if you start off with plate 1, time with God, He will give you the rest you need, and He even throws in some "me time" when He knows I need it most. God lays this out for us in Matthew 11:28, "Come to me all you who are weary and burdened and I will give you rest."

> "Come to me all you who are weary and burdened and I will give you rest."
>
> *-Matthew 11:28*

I am also fortunate to have a husband who understands the need for a periodic 'girls night out' as well. I have a wonderful group of supportive friends who gather regularly for coffee and chit-chat. We encourage one another, and support each other through our journey as women.

Now, looking back you can see that I have 12 plates spinning all at once usually, well 11 at best, and frankly, that's a tad overwhelming. Remember flexibility is the key ingredient in the homeschooling home.

The point isn't to be so rigid you're unable to divert from your schedule, but instead be flexible knowing that you have set God's priorities in place for your life, so that when a plate falls…and they will… it's not one of the big ones.

Chapter 23

Homeschool Burnout

Feeling burnout? It happens to the best of us...and I'd even venture to say that it happens to all of us at one time or another. It is commonly referred to as "homeschool burnout". The responsibilities of the homeschooling parent can be overwhelming at times, and the thought of another day or even another hour of homeschooling can seem like more than we can handle.

I once had someone tell me that moms who get burnt out just weren't serious enough about homeschooling. You can imagine how that affected me when I hit burnout that first year! The first thing I want to say is that "friend" was wrong.

The second thing I want to say is that feeling burnt out is totally normal. Unfortunately life isn't always a smooth sailing ship, and we can all get overwhelmed at times. Homeschool burnout happens to all of us at one point or another. The key is to learn how to overcome it.

Your child might be having a hard time with a particular subject, and your patience might be worn thin. Maybe a certain curriculum choice isn't working out as you'd originally planned. The thought of shipping your child off to school might have entered your mind once, twice, or even several times within the last few minutes.

> "Homeschool burnout happens to all of us at one point or another. The key is to learn how to overcome it."

There might also be outside factors that are making your homeschooling situation more difficult than normal, as well. The addition of a new baby, an illness, change of career, or moving to a new home can all contribute to a more than average stress level in the homeschooling parent.

If you are experiencing a form of burnout, there are things you can do to help minimize the stress you are feeling.

The first thing I suggest is to pray. Take some time to seek God in this moment and honestly listen to what His plan for your family is. Depending on your situation, a break might be in order, or maybe adjusting some of the things you are doing will help minimize the load.

Secondly, take inventory of things you *can* control. While certain things are out of our control, there are usually some things we can control to help with the situation. If you look closely there are probably outside factors that are contributing to your feeling of exhaustion. They might not even have anything to do with homeschooling at all.

For example over-scheduling activities, unrealistic expectations of yourself, over committing to things outside the home, trying to stick to an unrealistic schedule, lack of support, unrealistic expectations for your children, and trying to be super mom, can all cause us to eventually burnout. Take a look at the "Super Parent vs. Abiding Parent" chart on the following page to see which camp you fall in.

The good news is that homeschooling is flexible! We can modify our schedule if needed, or decrease the subjects we do each day. We can rearrange our daily load, adjust our lessons, or even cut back on their frequency if needed.

We can even switch to another curriculum if one is causing a particular amount of stress and anxiety for us.

Take some time to pray over the verses on the following pages and ask God to help you make any necessary changes so that you're abiding in His will for your family.

Super Parent	Abiding Parent
Does	Is (Psalm 46:10)
Tries to impress others	Pleases the Lord (Eph. 5:10, Proverbs 29:25)
Is controlled by an agenda	Is controlled by the Holy Spirit (Gal. 5:22-26)
Self-worth is found in their accomplishments	Self-worth is found in an accurate view of who you are in Christ Jesus (Eph. 2:10)
Peace is found in the "perfect" environment	Peace is found in Jesus in the midst of any storm (Is. 26:3)
Is discouraged by failure.	Failure reminds you that God's strength is made perfect in weakness. (2 Cor. 12:9-10)
Expects perfection from themselves as well as others	Practices grace with yourself and others. (Eph. 4:32)
Teaches their children to be good.	Teachers your children to be Godly. (Prov. 22:6)
Is frustrated with their lack of spiritual fruit.	Abides in Christ and bears much fruit. (John 15:5)
Does "activities" with their children.	Builds a relationship with their children. (Deut. 6:6-7)
Their perspective is based on what is seen.	Their perspective is based on what is unseen. (Col. 3:2)
Chooses quantity of activities.	Chooses the most excellent way. (1 Cor. 13)

Outside commitments

For me, one of the main reasons I have felt burnt out in my homeschooling journey has nothing to do with school at all. Instead it is an indirect effect from my outside commitments. You might be surprised to learn that decreasing some of your outside commitments can go a long way towards creating peace and harmony in your homeschool.

Homeschooling is demanding enough as it is, but having a full load of external demands will actually create dissention in your school even though they don't seem to be directly related. If we're constantly focusing on our other tasks that need to be done after school, we'll find ourselves rushing our students through things. They'll in turn be frustrated and discouraged, and we will ultimately become negative towards our homeschooling journey and ourselves, thinking we're not doing a good job.

Take time to access what is essential and what can be put on hold, or let go of for the year. As you progress, you will become more comfortable with homeschooling. Choosing priorities will also get easier as each year comes, so you might just need to make some minor adjustments to get through this year. Learn from your mistakes, and then re-access what you can do to help eliminate burnout next year.

Mid-year burnout

Another time I can usually count on a certain level of burnout is right after the Christmas season. During that time there is always such a great energy driving us. Everyone is excited for the upcoming holiday, people take breaks from school, enjoy time with family, and maybe even do fun unit studies that involve baking, crafts, and play dates.

Starting school back up in January after all that excitement can be less than enticing. And if you follow a typical August to June type schedule, you still have more than half way to go until summer break! I am not usually motivated to get back into the daily grind and neither are my children.

One fun way I've found to combat mid-year burnout is to introduce something new. I usually like to save a new unit study, something that is fun and exciting that my children can look forward to. I also like to pull out some new school supplies, and clean our desks before starting back up. Sometimes we even switch seats so everyone gets a "fresh" start for the New Year. We also like to re-decorate our room with a new theme, or get some new reward stickers to change things up a little bit. Never underestimate the small things, simple changes can make a positive impact when trying to revitalize your year!

Minimize distractions

I'm sure you've all heard it before, but one of the biggest frustrations in a homeschooling day is often unintentional outside distractions. Answering the phone, checking emails, texting friends, and generally being preoccupied with things other than school can all cause a certain amount of chaos to ensue.

Taking time to set boundaries with friends and family is a good way to help minimize distractions, and thus frustration between you and your children. Let your calls go to voicemail, or turn off the phone completely during school hours if it's too tempting to answer. I keep my cell phone on me in the event my husband calls, but otherwise I do my best to wait until after school time to take phone calls.

Another distraction that can draw you away is your computer. Don't be tempted to check your emails, Facebook, or any other online activities that might detract you from school.

When we allow ourselves to be distracted from school by these things, we model the level of commitment we expect out of our children. If we're not dedicated why should they be? And for that matter, why should they stay in their seats and work quietly while we chat away with a friend?

Not only that, but when we stop school to take a call, we fall behind in our day. Subjects might not be completed, things are left half-done, and work isn't checked. As we fall further and further behind after several unsuccessful days full of distractions, we can get to a point where we feel we can't ever catch up. This can commonly create a sense of failure in us and we can become discouraged and ultimately burnt out.

Now I'm not talking about emergency phone calls, certainly unexpected things can and will happen. And in some situations, students need to learn responsibility to be able to work if you need to step away. But for the most part, personal, non-emergency type calls and emails can wait until school is over.

Sleep, exercise, and nutrition

It goes without saying that sleep, proper exercise, and eating healthy is essential to combatting exhaustion and keeping a positive mental outlook. As hard as it may seem, make an effort to get to bed at a decent hour so you are able to get as close as possible to 8 hours of sleep each night. Going to bed early will not only help us rise earlier and prepare for our day. But it also helps tremendously with our patience when dealing with others.

Getting outside for a walk with your family is a good way to get a little extra fresh air and fit some exercise into your day. Not only is it great for you, but your children will appreciate a little time outside as well!

Review your priorities

Keeping God at the center of your homeschool is essential in staying the course. Analyze your priorities and make any adjustments necessary to make sure you are following His will for your homeschool. It might just be that your priorities got out of sync somewhere along the line.

At the start of this book I asked you to create a vision for your homeschool. Feeling homeschool burnout is the best time to revisit the vision you set forth for your homeschool. Take some time to review why you've chosen to homeschool, as well. Refocusing your energy towards why you are doing this is a great way to be refreshed and encouraged!

Chapter 24

Staying the Course & Naysayers

Staying the course in homeschooling can be difficult if you're not fully committed to this calling. There are several things that can cause a parent to doubt their choice to homeschool. In this chapter we'll discuss a few of the things that can discourage families from staying the course when homeschooling.

My intent is to encourage you to persevere through these trials and difficulties that will come. And I highly encourage you to pray for the Lord's leading as you begin each year.

Naysayers

There will always be those who may not support your decision to homeschool, and unfortunately they may also feel the need to express their opinions out loud. The best thing I've found to combat these people is to know why you are homeschooling in the first place. Stick to your vision and ignore everyone else. That said, if someone brings up a valid concern, take the time to address it within your family and make changes if necessary.

At the beginning of this book I mention creating a vision for your homeschool. Having your vision written down is particularly important when you start getting less than positive reactions to your new choice.

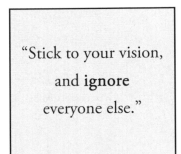

"Stick to your vision, and **ignore** everyone else."

Most likely you have chosen this path because you feel it is best for your family. Though it is easier said than done, sticking by this decision is vital to your homeschooling longevity. Having it written down is also helpful to reminding *you* why you've chosen this path. It's easy to start doubting your decision after hearing others' concerns. And if you have a solid standing on your choice to begin with, you are less likely to be swayed by others opinions.

And remember they are just those...opinions. If someone brings up something that is truly a concern for you, do your own research on the issue. Then make an educated decision on how to eliminate that concern from your homeschool.

Discouragement

The other issue that will come up at some point in your homeschooling journey is discouragement. We all get discouraged from time to time; we all have good days and bad days. And we've all seen the flashing lights of that yellow bus and considered for just a quick moment about putting our kids on it.

I want to encourage you...

Hang in there.

You are not alone.

Remember, tomorrow is a new day.

Don't give up.

Don't flag down the yellow bus.

Homeschooling is an eternally rewarding process, and the time and energy you have committed to devoting to your children's future won't return void. You might have days when it seems like nothing is going well, and your patience will be pushed to the limits.

But you'll also witness moments when your children are flourishing. You'll begin to see glimpses of where this journey is leading, and the benefits to your family will become apparent as well. As you witness the bonds created within your family, you'll be thankful that you took the leap. Homeschooling rewards come in baby steps, but you'll know when you see them, and they'll warm your heart and motivate you to persevere.

Here are some of the reasons that we have chosen to homeschool, and I have written them down so I can reflect upon them when I have discouraging days. You're welcome to use these as a guide, or come up with your own, but whatever your reasons for homeschooling are, write them down so they can encourage you in your journey.

1. **God:** The number one reason we homeschool is this; *I am called*. Really I could stop here. I remember about seven years ago, we found ourselves at a bible study for married couples. The hosts

leading the study were a homeschooling family. I walked in and saw their room, all the fun "school stuff", then met their wonderfully awesome family and immediately stated "I WANT TO HOMESCHOOL!" She politely reminded me that maybe I should have some children first. Well, God clearly took care of that for us, blessing us with four children.

When we first started homeschooling, I wasn't totally on board. It was a fun thing I did just until "real school" started. But as we progressed and prayed on it, I believe God laid out the answer for us in His Word.

- *Ephesians 6:4* states: "Fathers, do not exasperate your children; instead, bring them up in the training and instruction of the Lord."

- *Deuteronomy 4:9* says "Only be careful, and watch yourselves closely so that you do not forget the things your eyes have seen or let them slip from your heart as long as you live. Teach them to your children and to their children after them."

- *Proverbs 1:7* "The fear of the Lord is the beginning of knowledge."

- *Deuteronomy 6:5-7* says "Love the LORD your God with all your heart and with all your soul and with all your strength. These commandments that I give you today are to be upon your hearts. Impress them on your children. Talk about them when you sit at home and when you walk along the road, when you lie down and when you get up."

This last one stuck with me because I wondered to myself, how am I to teach my children when we sit at home, when we walk along the road, when we lie down and when we get up if they are gone all day long? How can I hide God's word in their heart if most of the opportunities happen when they are at school? How can I truly impress upon their hearts if I only see them at dinner and at bedtime?

- 2 Cor 10:5 says "…bringing every thought into captivity to the obedience of Christ"

How can I make sure they learn to bring every thought captive to Christ if they are spending 80% of their day with someone else?

- *Isaiah 38:19* - "The living, the living–they praise you, as I am doing today; fathers tell their children about your faithfulness."
- *Luke 6:40* - "A student is not above his teacher, but everyone who is fully trained will be like his teacher." Which teacher do I want them to be like?

- *Romans 12:2* - "And do not be conformed to this world, but be transformed by the renewing of your mind, that you may prove what is that good and acceptable and perfect will of God."

I had to let go of preconceived notions of what I thought homeschooling looked like and realize that I do not answer to this world, but to Christ. Again, it came down to my time and my priorities; how can I teach my kids if they are not with me during the everyday ordinary comings and goings?

2. **Opportunity:** The opportunities for spiritual, character, academic, social, and family time when homeschooling are AWESOME! I truly believe the traditional American family is disintegrating. It's too easy to get caught up in the business of this world, running from one activity to the next ... or whatever takes up our time.

We can become so busy running around we forget to actually spend time together. Homeschooling affords our family the precious commodity of time. Time spent together, and frankly that's really what our kids want from us, our time. It breaks my heart when I hear people say they can't wait for school to start again, as if their kids are burdens. I sometimes feel that if my kids were in school I could get so much done! But I'm quickly reminded that 'me time' isn't in the Bible, well it is, it's just referred to as 'selfishness'.

Then I am reminded how quickly time passes, and how few years we have our children with us before they move on to their own lives. If the average person lives say 85 years, then the 18 years our kids spend with us is less than 1/4 of their lives. I don't want to look back and think I didn't spend enough time with them, and 3 hours a day just isn't enough for me.

3. **Academically:** speaking homeschoolers typically rate 37 percentage points higher than public school students. The average homeschool 8th grade student performs four grade levels above the national average (Rudner study). At home, I can make sure we have mastery of subjects, go at the right pace for each child, we have one-on-one (not one-on-twenty) teaching, and I can tailor my curriculum to their needs.

4. **Social:** So that leaves me with my social reservations. I still struggle with the idea of this sometimes, and we have debated it over and over. I think I misunderstand the word "socialization" as

the notion that spending time with 30 other 6 year olds is in some way benefiting my child. I challenge you to visit your local middle school, junior high, or high school, walk down the hallways, and tell me which behavior you see that you would like your child to emulate.

Just to be clear, I looked up the word 'socialization' and found some disturbing things. I do not want to 'convert or adapt my children to the needs of society'. I *do* want them to be able to function in our society, but as Christians we are in this world, but not of this world.

I do think children need to spend time with friends, and we *have* committed to making sure our kids are involved in enough 'outside the home' activities like sports, dance, church, and homeschooling co-ops that we are confident that the amount of time our kids spend with others their same age is appropriate. Not too many activities though, we still focus on our family time as a priority. After the first year of homeschooling I think we were "over-socialized"!

Considering my opinion means nothing, which it doesn't, I think it's more important to ask ourselves what the bible says about socialization.

- *Proverbs 22: 24-25* - "Do not make friends with the hot-tempered, do not associate with those who are easily angered; or you may learn their ways and get yourself ensnared."
- *1 Corinthians 15:33* - Do not be misled: "bad company corrupts good character."

5. Our Goals: We asked ourselves "What do we want our children to look like when they've finished their formal education?

In Luke 2:52 it says "And Jesus grew in wisdom and in stature, and in favor with God and men."

We want our children to learn to trust in the Word of God, and to have it hidden in their heart. We want to train them in the way they should go, so it may go *well* with them. We want them to be healthy, confident, and to know they are beautifully and wonderfully made. We want them to keep their childlike faith, and we want them to be a light in this world. We want them to "always be prepared to give an answer to everyone who asks [them] to give the reason for the hope that [they] have. But do this with gentleness and respect." (1 Pet 3:15) We want them to be confident, to have good manners, to be compassionate, to be respectful, and to be humble in spirit.

That's a tall order for a teacher, and frankly I'm not sure they'd be able to comply at our local school. Honestly, I'm not sure I can do it either, but I'd rather trust God to work through **us** than leave it up to a stranger.

Lastly, and on a more selfish note, we can protect their innocence a tad longer. We don't have to deal with peer pressure. Our children still like Clifford and Curious George. They don't wear suggestive clothing or makeup because everyone else does, they don't beg me for a Wii or an iPhone, and they don't look down on their younger siblings because they aren't cool anymore.

We don't have to worry about car-pool, unhealthy lunches, or poor teachers. And my personal favorite, we don't have to get up at 6am every day to get out of the house for school! *(This alone is enough to keep me homeschooling!)*

But these are the goals set forth by our family's needs. Your family may be different, and your reasons for homeschooling will be as well. The point is to be committed to your choice and persevere through your calling.

Thank you so much for reading Homeschooling 101!

I hope it was helpful to your journey as a homeschooling family. As always, feel free to contact me if you have any questions at erica@confessionsofahomeschooler.com.

Have a wonderful homeschooling journey!

Appendix

Along with your Homeschooling 101 book purchase, you also receive a free copy of my Homeschooling Lesson Planner and Forms!

Follow the instructions below to download a pdf version of my homeschooling forms and a free lesson planner!

- Visit: store.confessionsofahomeschooler.com
- Click on "Planners", then "Lesson Planner – Colorful".
- Add the item to your cart and use coupon code: HOMESchooling_101

The Homeschooling 101 Forms download includes:

- ❖ Our Vision Statement
- ❖ Notice of Intent Form
- ❖ Household Rules Chart
- ❖ Behavior & Discipline Chart
- ❖ Our Family Schedule
- ❖ Our Commitment Worksheet
- ❖ Our Curriculum
- ❖ Curriculum Plan Overview
- ❖ Weekly Subject Overview
- ❖ Weekly Schedule Overview

- ❖ Our Book List
- ❖ Planned Field Trips
- ❖ Extra-Curricular Activities
- ❖ Crafts Supply List
- ❖ School Supply Shopping List
- ❖ Photocopies Needed
- ❖ Unit Study Planner
- ❖ Preschool Assessment Form
- ❖ Kindergarten Assessment Form
- ❖ Sight Word Assessment Form
- ❖ Homeschool Attendance Records
- ❖ Homeschool Long Term Grade Record
- ❖ Super Mom vs. Abiding Mom
- ❖ Year at-a-Glance Calendars
- ❖ Printable Lesson Planner FREE!
- ❖ Resources & Links

Resources & Links

Chapter 1

- Homeschool Legal Defense Association: www.hslda.org
- Notice of Intent to Homeschool Form: www.confessionsofahomeschooler.com/blog/2012/06/notice-of-intent-to-homeschool-form.html
- Standardized Testing: www.confessionsofahomeschooler.com/blog/2011/08/standardized-testing-your-homeschooler.html
- Core Standards: www.corestandards.org
- Chore Chart: www.confessionsofahomeschooler.com/blog/2011/01/chore-chart-cards.html

Chapter 2

- www.homeschoolreviews.com
- www.welltrainedmind.com
- simplycharlottemason.com
- www.montessori.edu

Art:

- World's Greatest Artists 1: store.confessionsofahomeschooler.com
- World's Greatest Artists 2: store.confessionsofahomeschooler.com
- Artistic Pursuits: www.artisticpursuits.com
- Evans, Joy, Skelton, Tanya. *How To Teach Art to Children*, Grades 1-6. Evan-Moor 2001
- Deep Space Sparkle: www.deepspacesparkle.com
- Draw Write Now: www.drawyourworld.com

Bible:

- Character Studies: www.confessionsofahomeschooler.com
- Grape Vine Studies: www.grapevinestudies.com/?AffId=9
- What's in the Bible: www.zfer.us/Wuc9j
- Abeka: www.abeka.com
- Answers For Kids: www.answersingenesis.org

Handwriting:

- Abeka: www.abeka.com
- A Reason for Handwriting: www.areasonfor.com
- Handwriting without Tears: www.hwtears.com
- BJU Press: www.bjupresshomeschool.com

Health/Fitness:

- Abeka: www.abeka.com
- Family Time Fitness:
  www.1shoppingcart.com/app/?af=1381011

Math:

- Math U See: www.mathusee.com
- Saxon: saxonpublishers.hmhco.com
- Teaching Textbooks: www.teachingtextbooks.com

Music:

- Greatest Composers: store.confessionsofahomeschooler.com
- Piano is Easy: www.pianoiseasy2.com
- Maestro Classics: maestroclassics.com

Science:

- Abeka: www.abeka.com
- Scientists & Inventors Units:
  store.confessionsofahomeschooler.com
- Apologia Science: www.apologia.com
- God's Design: www.answersingenesis.org
- NaturExplorers: shiningdawnbooks.com

Spelling:

- Abeka: www.abeka.com
- All About Spelling: allaboutlearningpress.net/go.php?id=202

English/Grammar:

- Abeka: www.abeka.com
- BJU Press: www.bjupresshomeschool.com
- Easy Grammar: www.easygrammar.com
- Rod & Staff English: www.milestonebooks.com
- Wordly Wise: www.wordlywise3000.com

Foreign Language:

- Rosetta Stone: www.rosettastone.com
- PowerSpeak: www.powerspeak.com

History/Geography:

- Abeka: www.abeka.com
- BJU Press: www.bjupresshomeschool.com
- Expedition Earth World Geography: store.confessionsofahomeschooler.com
- Road Trip USA Geography: store.confessionsofahomeschooler.com
- Mystery of History: www.themysteryofhistory.info
- Time Travelers: www.homeschoolinthewoods.com

Literature:

- Classical Literature Units: store.confessionsofahomeschooler.com
- Hunt, Gladys. *Honey for a Child's Heart*. Zondervan, 2002.
- Clarkson, Sarah. *Read for the Heart.* Apologia Press, 2009.

Preschool:

- Letter of the Week: www.confessionsofahomeschooler.com/letter-of-the-week
- Before 5 in a Row: fiveinarow.com

Reading/Phonics:

- Abeka: www.abeka.com
- BJU Press: www.bjupresshomeschool.com
- All About Reading: allaboutlearningpress.net/go.php?id=202
- Explode the Code: www.explodethecode.com

Typing:

- Typing Instructor: www.typinginstructor.com
- Typing Web: www.typingweb.com

Writing:

- WriteShop: www.writeshop.com
- Excellence in Writing: www.excellenceinwriting.com

Chapter 3

- Rainbow Resource Center: www.rainbowresource.com
- Christian Book: www.christianbook.com
- Amazon: www.amazon.com
- eBay: www.ebay.com
- Homeschool Classifieds: www.homeschoolclassifieds.com

Chapter 4

- Teach Them Diligently: www.teachthemdiligently.net
- Great Homeschool Conventions: www.greathomeschoolconventions.com
- Homeschool Conventions: www.homeschoolconventions.com
- Homeschooling vision worksheet: www.confessionsofahomeschooler.com/blog/2011/02/10-days-of-homeschooling-enrichment-day.html

Chapter 5

- Donna Young Blue Calendars: donnayoung.org
- Homeschool laws by state: www.hslda.org
- Homeschool Tracker: www.homeschooltracker.com
- Planbook: www.hellmansoft.com

- My Lesson Planners: store.confessionsofahomeschooler.com
- Well Planned Day Planner: hedua.com
- Weekly Homeschool Planner: www.e-junkie.com/ecom/gb.php?cl=141844&c=ib&aff=169520
- Our Curriculum: www.confessionsofahomeschooler.com/blog/tag/our-curriculum
- Our Schedule: www.confessionsofahomeschooler.com/blog/2009/10/whats-typical-day-like.html
- Our Schoolroom: www.confessionsofahomeschooler.com/blog/2011/08/our-schoolroom-on-ikea.html
- YouTube Channel: www.youtube.com/user/EricasHomeschool

Chapter 6

- YouTube Channel: www.youtube.com/user/EricasHomeschool
- Workbox System: www.confessionsofahomeschooler.com/blog/tag/the-workbox-system
- Workbox Video Tutorial: www.confessionsofahomeschooler.com/blog/2013/01/workbox-system-video-tutorial.html

- Homeschool Supplies:
  www.confessionsofahomeschooler.com/blog/2013/01/homesch
  ool-supplies-organization.html

More helpful links on organization:

- Homeschool Supply List:
  www.confessionsofahomeschooler.com/blog/2012/05/homesch
  ool-supply-list.html
- Preschool Supply List:
  www.confessionsofahomeschooler.com/blog/2010/09/supply-
  list-for-letter-of-week.html
- Preschool Products We Love:
  www.confessionsofahomeschooler.com/blog/2010/01/preschool
  -things-we-love.html
- Alphabet Desk Mate:
  www.confessionsofahomeschooler.com/blog/2011/11/alphabet-
  desk-mate.html
- Math-U-See Block Organizer:
  www.confessionsofahomeschooler.com/blog/2009/09/math-u-
  see-block-organizer.html
- Homemade Pom-pom magnets:
  www.confessionsofahomeschooler.com/blog/2012/09/homema
  de-pom-pom-magnets-2.html

Chapter 8

- Daily Learning Notebook:
  www.confessionsofahomeschooler.com/blog/tag/daily-learning-notebook
- Calendar Time:
  www.confessionsofahomeschooler.com/blog/2010/04/calendar-time.html

Chapter 11

- Educational iPad Apps:
  www.confessionsofahomeschooler.com/blog/tag/ipad-apps
- LeapFrog: Letter Factory DVD, 2009.
- LeapFrog: Talking Words Factory, 2009.
- Leapfrog: Numberland, 2012.
- Leapfrog: Adventures in Shapeville Park, 2013.
- LeapFrog: Math Circus DVD, 2010.

Chapter 12

- Letter of the Week Preschool Curriculum:
  store.confessionsofahomeschooler.com

- Things we love: Preschool Edition: www.confessionsofahomeschooler.com/blog/2010/01/preschool-things-we-love.html
- Educational iPad Apps for Preschoolers: www.confessionsofahomeschooler.com/blog/category/ipad-apps
- Before Five in a Row: www.fiveinarow.com
- Beechick, Ruth. *The Three R's*. Mott Media, 2006.
- LeapFrog Educational DVDs: www.leapfrog.com
- Meredith, Susan. *Usborne Science in the Kitchen*. Usborne Publishing, 2007.
- Edom, Helen. *Usborne Science with Water*. Usborne Publishing, 2007.

Chapter 13

- Notebooking Pages: notebookingpages.com
- Notebooking Fairy: www.e-junkie.com/ecom/gb.php?cl=142669&c=ib&aff=169520
- Homeschool Share: www.homeschoolshare.com
- File Folder Games: www.filefolderfun.com
- Field Trips
- Museum Trips

- Reading Incentives:
  www.confessionsofahomeschooler.com/blog/2012/11/homeschool-reading-incentives.html
- Educational iPad Apps:
  www.confessionsofahomeschooler.com/blog/category/ipad-apps
- Artist Studies: store.confessionsofahomeschooler.com
- Composer Studies: store.confessionsofahomeschooler.com
- Hands On World Geography:
  store.confessionsofahomeschooler.com
- Hands on United States Geography:
  store.confessionsofahomeschooler.com
- Scientists & Inventors Units:
  store.confessionsofahomeschooler.com
- Classic Literature Units: store.confessionsofahomeschooler.com
- Time Traveler Units: www.homeschoolinthewoods.com
- Nature Studies: www.shiningdawnbooks.com

Chapter 14

- HSLDA Homeschooling High school: www.hslda.org
- FastWeb.com: www.fastweb.com - A great resource for homeschooling through high school and preparing college bound students.
- The Home Scholar: www.thehomescholar.com
- Donna Young High School Forms: www.donnayoung.org

- Cohen, Cafi. Homeschooling the Teen Years Prima Publishing, May 11, 2000.

Chapter 15

- Homeschool Classifieds: www.homeschoolclassifieds.com
- eBay: www.eBay.com
- Local Used Curriculum Fairs *(Do an internet search for used fairs in your area.)*
- Half Price Books: www.hpb.com
- Half.Com: www.half.ebay.com
- Amazon: www.amazon.com
- Christian Book: www.christianbook.com
- Rainbow Resource: www.rainbowresource.com

Free Homeschooling Resources:

- Confessions of a Homeschooler: www.confessionsofahomeschooler.com
- Deep Space Sparkle: www.deepspacesparkle.com
- Donna Young: www.donnayoung.org
- Homeschool Share: www.homeschoolshare.com
- KB Teachers: www.kbteachers.com
- Lapbook Lessons: www.lapbooklessons.com
- Ambleside Online: www.amblesideonline.org

- Homeschool Freebie of the Day:
  www.homeschoolfreebie.wholesomechildhood.com
- Starfall: www.starfall.com
- Spelling City: www.spellingcity.com

Chapter 18

- Awanas: www.awana.org

Chapter 20

- Autism Speaks: www.autismspeaks.org
- Dianne Craft: www.diannecraft.org
- Family Education: www.school.familyeducation.com
- Handwriting Without Tears: www.hwtears.com
- HSLDA: www.hslda.org
- Laureate Special Needs Software: www.laureatelearning.com
- List of National Organizations: www.hslda.org
- NATHHAN: www.nathhan.com
- NHEN: www.nhen.org
- NorCal Center on Deafness, Inc: www.norcalcenter.org
- PACE: www.tckconsultant.org
- Sensory Processing Disorder Foundation:
  www.spdfoundation.net

- Special Needs Homeschooling: www.networkedblogs.com

Chapter 21

- Homeschool Statistics from www.hslda.org

Chapter 22

- Daily Audio Bible: www.dailyaudiobible.com
- Kids Daily Audio Bible: www.dailyaudiobible.com
- Monthly Meal Planner: www.confessionsofahomeschooler.com/blog/tag/monthly-meal-plan
- Freezer Meals: www.confessionsofahomeschooler.com/blog/2010/05/freezer-meals-cooking-twice-month.html
- My Monthly Meal Planning: www.confessionsofahomeschooler.com/blog/tag/monthly-meal-plan
- eMeals: e-mealz.com/amember/go.php?r=252457&i=b3
- Once A Month Cooking: www.once-a-month-cookingworld.com
- Crockpot Recipes: www.southernfood.about.com
- The Fly Lady: www.flylady.net

Chapter 23

- Super Parent vs. Abiding Parent: written by Renee Hirsch, used with permission, and modified for use in this book.

Visit Confessions of a Homeschooler

- Website: www.confessionsofahomeschooler.com
- Email: erica@confessionsofahomeschooler.com
- Facebook: www.facebook.com/ConfessionsofaHomeschooler
- Pinterest: pinterest.com/ericahomeschool
- Twitter: twitter.com/ericahomeschool
- YouTube: www.youtube.com/user/EricasHomeschool

About the author

Erica Arndt is a Christian, a wife, and a homeschooling mom to four wonderful children. She authors the top rated homeschooling website www.confessionsofahomeschooler.com

There she offers free printables, resources, ideas, and a variety of homeschool curriculum. She enjoys spending time with family and friends, and dabbles in graphic design in her "free" time. Stop by her site for a visit!